What If God Is Like This?

Meet the God You've Never Known

Will Hathaway

www.will-hathaway.com

Creative Team Publishing
San Diego

© 2011 by Will Hathaway.

All rights reserved. No part of this book may be reproduced, stored in a retrieval system or transmitted in any form or by any means without the prior written permission of the publisher, except by a reviewer who may quote brief passages in a review to be distributed through electronic media, or printed in a newspaper, magazine or journal.

Permissions and Credits:

Scripture references taken from the HOLY BIBLE, NEW INTERNATIONAL VERSON. Copyright 1973, 1978, 1984 by International Bible Society. Used by permission of Zondervan. All rights reserved.
Blue Letter Bible. "Dictionary and Word Search for *egkataleip (Strong's 1459)*". Blue Letter Bible. 1996-2011. 30 Jul 2011., http://www.blueletterbible.org/lang/lexicon/lexicon.cfm?Strongs=G1459&t=KJV
A variety of stories are presented in the book to illustrate concepts and points about God's interaction with mankind. All the stories are true. Some of these are direct accounts for which permission was obtained for their use. Others for which permission was not obtained employ fictitious characters and events in order to protect the identities of those involved. Any resemblance to actual names of people, situations, companies or events is purely coincidental.
Story of the mountain lion used with permission of Jose Zambrano.
Story of Steve Courteol used with permission of Steve Courteol.
Story of Megan Fowler used with permission of Megan Fowler.
Story of Paul Hathaway used with permission of Paul Hathaway.
Stanley Milgram, Milgram Experiment in 1961 reference quoted with permission of Shuttleworth, Martyn (2008). Milgram Experiment Ethics. Retrieved 07/21/2011 from Experiment Resources http://www.experiment-resources.com/milgram-experiment-ethics.html
Albert Camus quote used with permission of "Albert Camus." 1-Famous-Quotes.com. Gledhill Enterprises, 2011. Sat Jul 16 21:55:38 2011. http://www.1-famous-quotes.com/quote/70024

ISBN: 978-0-9838919-3-2
PUBLISHED BY CREATIVE TEAM PUBLISHING
www.CreativeTeamPublishing.com
San Diego
Printed in the United States of America

Endorsements

Will Hathaway's *What If God Is Like This?* speaks right to the heart of profound questions being asked within our culture about God, His characteristics and purposes, and our roles and responses to Him in the midst of the freedom He gives. Very few books have recently challenged me to "work out my faith" like this one has.

~Andy Frank, Worship Artist, Songwriter, and Producer

In my almost 20 years of ministry and following the Lord I have come to realize how few answers I truly have about God. In fact I now recognize that I have many more questions than I have answers. Many times I don't even realize I have those questions; I just know that my heart longs for more. This book does a phenomenal job at getting to those questions and peeling away the layers to get at truth.

~ Chris McGuire, Area Director, Burbank Young Life

Will offers a refreshingly genuine reminder that it is not only okay to ask difficult questions, it's necessary. *What if God is Like This?* traces Will's quest to search out the truth as he raises questions we have all had, and seeks to both answer and understand them.

~ **Derek Turner, Founder, The World By Sea Charities, www.theworldbysea.com**

Will has captured what most people think during their personal relationship with God and our quest to find Him. He eloquently raised the issue that the world is not perfect and God doesn't expect us to be, either, which is inspiring. God has given us the gift of free will and the responsibilities that come with this gift. In the end, God hopes we choose Him.

~ **Randy Robbins, Former Defensive Back for the Denver Broncos and New England Patriots**

What If God Is Like This?

Meet the God You've Never Known

Will Hathaway

www.will-hathaway.com

Table of Contents

Dedication	9
Who Is God and What Is He Really Like?	11
1 What If God Isn't the Only Thing Supernatural?	15
2 What If God's Greatest Desire for Us Is Not Obedience?	27
3 The Result of Freedom	45
4 What If God Is Dealing with a Personal Crisis?	51
5 What If Hell Wasn't Created for People?	61
6 What If Some Things Are Hard for God?	71
7 What If God Has His Hands Full?	83
8 What If Salvation Is Not Standardized?	91
9 The Big Decision	107
10 What If God Has a Treasure?	115
11 True Love	119
12 A Return to Freedom	129
Conclusion	137
Acknowledgements	141
The Author	143
Speaking Engagements and Products	147

Dedication

I dedicate this book to everyone who has ever had doubts about God but was afraid to admit them. This book is for those who have asked questions they feel haven't been adequately answered, particularly regarding Christianity. This book is for those who feel imprisoned by life, their situation, their experiences, and their fears. This book is for those who want to meet the God they believed was there, but have not yet experienced.

I dedicate this book to my dad and mom.
- Dad, thanks for writing your books and inspiring me to write mine. Thanks for teaching me that it's okay to think outside the box. Finally, thanks for stopping the truck.
- Mom, thanks for your constant encouragement. Thanks for the example you set for me.

I dedicate this book to my wife, Karra. Karra, thank you for entertaining my crazy ideas. Thanks for being a great wife and a great friend.

Who Is God and What Is He Really Like?

Who is God? What is He really like? Do you ever ask those questions? Obviously every religion has their teachings about Him and most people have their opinions about Him, but overall it's really just speculation.

Do you ever wonder who He genuinely is, His true personality, His true nature? If we could peer behind the drapery of this realm and take a peek into His existence, what would we find? Or more importantly, who would we find?

A friend of mine once told me that it seems like everybody has different thoughts on God, but ultimately what you and I think really doesn't matter anyway. If He's real, He is who

He is — what we think we know doesn't affect anything. But how is it, when it comes to the most important being in the universe that there can be so much ambiguity and so many different positions about Him and what His character is?

If we pay attention to some religious teachers we can be persuaded to believe that God is some sort of egotistical monster, an all-powerful creature that appears highly insecure in His demands for our allegiance and worship. Or, He may be perceived as one that enjoys imposing unlimited power on a humanity that is helpless to restrain Him. Others choose to believe that there is no God at all and can make a good argument for such an opinion.

When we witness atrocities inflicted upon blameless people or the suffering of innocent children, some may have to question the existence of God, or at least the existence of a *good* God. When we watch evil abound, observe the reality of cancer and other debilitating diseases, witness severe drought, devastating famine, earthquakes, and other natural disasters, some of us quickly begin to question the characteristics of this benevolent, all knowing, all-powerful, and ever present being.

We might deduce that if He is really all-powerful then He must be completely uncaring to allow such things to take place. Or, if He really is caring then He must not be all-powerful, lacking the strength to prevent the anguish and evil that exist in our world.

Religion often teaches us that God is a finicky creature who must be obeyed at all costs. He is quick to fire lightning bolts at those who fail to follow His decrees and damns to an everlasting Hell even those who may be *good* but refuse to *believe* the *right* things.

Is this really what God is like?

Others preach that God is a cosmic teddy bear, a loving deity that would rather be our buddy than anything else. Still, some say that He is a clock maker, an emotionless personality that created the universe, set it in motion, and then left it to its own devices. In this view He appears distant, unreasonable, and cold, while at the same time we are taught that "God is love." The incongruity of all of this is unsettling and unnerving to say the least.

As a result of His mysterious existence we humans are often left confused by our world and His ways. When things are going well we seem to be more willing to discuss the possibility of God. Sometimes, when something dramatically positive happens in our lives, such as dodging that car in the intersection, our sports team winning a game, or that girl actually calling back, we might utter the words, "Thank God!" Yet for the most part, even if we do believe in Him, we go about our business, be it eating, sleeping, working, or playing, simply ignoring Him.

Normally it is only when things go wrong that we grant Him our attention. That attention often takes the form of pleading for His help at best and cursing Him for our misfortune or denying He even exists at worst. Many will admit not knowing much about Him but that doesn't stop us from jumping to conclusions. There are countless possibilities as to who God may be, and what God may be like. Join me in asking this question: What if He is like this?

1
What If God Isn't the Only Thing Supernatural?

Would a supernatural creature existing in a supernatural world recognize that world as such?

"It's a lion," said the old cowboy as he pointed from his horse to a paw print in the sandy wash. With wide eyes I looked at the large cat print and then nervously began to scan the walls of the canyon on either side of our position. My horse jerked its head up, startling me before I realized it was simply annoyed with a fly buzzing around its eyes.

It was summertime, school was out and I was spending my days on the family ranch working as a cowhand with Jose, our ranch foreman. At fourteen years old, I still had a lot to learn, especially about observing animal tracks.

Jose and I were riding in a remote part of the ranch looking for stray cattle when we came across the evidence of the big cat. Although somewhat rare, mountain lions in that part of Southern Arizona can reach up to 150 pounds and, based on the size of the print, this one was rather large. The impression was still fresh; Jose estimated a day or so.

Neither one of us had a firearm, so as we continued up the canyon I kept a close eye on the dogs. I figured they would be the first to sense the presence of a lion should we cross paths or come close. Jose kept his eyes to the ground following the evidence left behind by the predator as we moved onward. I already knew Jose was one of the best trackers I had ever met, but I was about to discover just how good he really was. With his sun darkened skin and weathered features, he peered out from under his beat-up cowboy hat and pointed occasionally to other tracks as we proceeded. I would then strain with my untrained eyes to pick them out from the lumps and bumps in the thick sand.

After traveling about a quarter of a mile we came to a solid cement wall ascending ten to twelve feet straight out of the canyon bed. This wall was the remnant of an old dam that had been built somewhere around 1930 to provide water for cattle in the area. Over the years the canyon would flood with the monsoon rains and eventually the sediment filled the unmaintained obstruction to the top, creating a man-made waterfall whenever the water would run. The remainder of the year the canyon was empty and dry, baking in the hot Sonora Desert.

As we approached this strange looking wall, I was under the impression Jose had gone back to following the tracks of the cattle we were looking for, when he told me to move toward the bank of the wash. He then got off his horse and began intensely probing the ground. To me it was just a sandy canyon bottom, but to Jose this area was telling a story. It was as if he was reading the pages of a book. I could see he was getting excited.

After looking at the ground for a few minutes he told me to get off my horse and to carefully walk over to him, minding where I stepped as I approached. He then began to voice aloud the silent story contained in the sand. About thirty feet west of the cement wall he pointed out a set of hoof shaped prints belonging to a small deer. He said that sometime last night or very early on this morning the lion had been perched at the top of the old dam. He then pointed to two small mounds of sand at the base of the dam where the front paws of the lion had landed, scooping the dirt up as the large animal had hit the ground. The deer had made a futile attempt to flee but the effort was too little, too late. Spattered sand and giant paw prints documented the final moments of the small creature's life.

We mounted our horses again and started heading back

out of the canyon from the direction we had come. About 150 yards downstream Jose directed his horse to the left and began climbing a steep canyon wall filled with sage brush and small gnarled oak trees. The horses grunted and stumbled up the side of the hill and the dirt gave way beneath their feet with every other step. It was rugged, rocky, foreboding. We climbed 30-40 feet above the canyon floor before Jose suddenly stopped, got off his horse, and walked through the scrub along the edge of the steep incline. He used his hands to push aside a small mound of leaves at the base of several small trees. He took hold of one leaf, and when he pulled on it the entire mound moved. My stomach sank when I realized that the leaf he had pulled was not a leaf at all. It was an ear. He lifted up the head of a deer up from the leaves. It was the carcass of the lion's kill! He then quickly set the deer back in place and covered it back up with leaves, being careful to leave little of his scent behind. He then looked at me intensely and said, "Vámonos!" (Let's go!), as he climbed on his horse. "No argument here," I thought to myself. I was already eager to leave before our hungry friend returned to finish feeding.

I will never forget the awe I felt during that entire experience. Looking back I'm still amazed at how Jose was able to tell so much from what seemed like so little. As with so many things in life, it took a trained eye to know what to look for, to crack the code in the sand, and unlock its story.

What if God is Like This?

I haven't gotten much better at tracking over the years but thanks to that experience I've learned that many times plenty of evidence is right in front of me. The key is whether or not my eye is trained enough to recognize it. Sometimes the obvious is not just what we think we see in front of us. The truth can also be about what's not there as well.

Take the atom, for instance. I find its existence fascinating. How is it possible that the most powerful of weapons can be made on the premise of such a tiny particle? I'm sure great scientific minds could explain the process to me but that would only lead to growing frustration on their part because I'm not sure I'm capable of understanding that kind of scientific depth.

I still remember sitting in one of my junior high school science classes when the teacher, Mr. Courteol, walked up to the brick wall at the front of the classroom and slapped it with his open hand. After hearing the smack echo through the room, he turned to us and explained that the wall he struck was mostly "not there." I figured he was just kidding with us as he did possess an odd sense of humor. After all he was a junior high school science teacher! However, he went on to explain that everything is made up of atoms and atoms for the most part are composed of empty space. He taught us that at the center of every atom is the nucleus. It's made up of protons and neutrons. Racing around the nucleus, like planets around a star, are the electrons. Nothing exists between the nucleus and the electrons. It's simply empty space that makes up the volume of the atom. In fact, according to the physics department at Georgia State University, if the nucleus of a gold atom was one foot in radius, the outer layer of electrons would be 3.3 miles away!

View the site, http://hyperphysics.phy-astr.gsu.edu/hbase/nuclear/nucuni.html. That is a lot of empty space!

It is for this reason, Mr. Courteol explained, that most of the space the wall occupied was actually empty. The same was true for not only the wall but for everything else in the universe, from the densest lead to the very body you possess. So next time you meet someone who seems a little off and you say, "Man, that guy just isn't all there…" well, you're right! Since everything is made up of atoms, everything mostly is "not there."

One very personal obstacle to Christianity that I've wrestled with throughout my life was the belief that God even existed to begin with. I had been taught about Him from birth but as I got older I began to wonder why I never saw this awesome being and why He would spend so much of His time hiding from me.

I work with a friend who is an atheist. He is certain that God does not exist. He recently asked me what it was that assured me of my faith. As someone raised in the church, now serving as a pastor, the answer should have come easily, but in reality it caused me to do a great deal of soul searching. As one who has struggled with beliefs about God, I know what it's like to be frustrated by people who seem to have their faith come to them easily. I've never been one to rely on shallow Sunday school answers that appear to only apply to those who have a church background.

I am the type of person who likes things that are tangible. I have to see it to believe it. I can't tell you how many times I have prayed for God to allow me to experience something *supernatural* to solidify my faith. I was jealous of the ancient followers who got to see storms silenced, mighty prison walls collapse, and normal men walking in a fiery furnace unscathed. Why didn't I get to experience watching the lame leap, the blind receive sight, or the dead rise? I would even promise God that if I could just experience *any* of these wonders even a *single* time, I would not be like those in the Bible who quickly lost their faith after witnessing something as amazing as the parting of the Red Sea. I would try to take solace in the words of Jesus to Thomas, "…blessed are those who have not seen and yet have believed." (John 20:29) Those words, however, were of little comfort for me. I still felt I would rather be part of the *less blessed* crowd if it meant I actually got to see something supernatural. That way if someone were ever to ask me what gave me my faith, I could easily reference the time I saw food multiplied or the sun stand still.

So there I sat, locking eyes with my friend who was patiently awaiting my answer. As I collected my thoughts, my mind returned to a past conversation where I had asked this same question to another friend of mine, a man for whom I have a great deal of admiration and respect. His response was simple: "Where did everything come from?" This was something that I had heard many times, but for some reason this time it clicked differently. He left it at that, but his question sent my mind racing down a path that would eventually guide me to a solid, tangible answer to this very relevant query. It would also finally lead to the fulfillment of my prayer: to experience the supernatural and give me what I needed to anchor my faith!

In order to fully appreciate the supernatural, one must first ask the question, "What is natural?" I think most us would describe the natural world as that which we can see, taste, touch, smell, and hear. Interestingly, this view is exactly what kept me from experiencing the supernatural.

Let's take a moment and imagine we are in a remote desert area, miles from the nearest city. We are out for a stroll on a dark moonless night and peer up into the heavens. What do we see? Do we see the stars scattered across the night sky like salt thrown on a black tablecloth? Can we see the Milky Way and the Big Dipper? Look at it all! There is so much out there!

What if God is Like This?

Or is there?

For as much as we can see there is far more that we cannot see. In between each of those sparkling specks are trillions and trillions of miles of nothing, just empty darkness, cold and void. Space, as its very name implies, is mainly just an immense nothing. Interesting isn't it? Those gigantic galaxies we see swirling out in the expanse of space are really not all that different than the tiniest of atoms. They appear to be a solid mass of whirling stars, but in reality they are mostly empty space.

Scientists tell us that billions and billions of years ago a huge explosion created everything. But a question that I have never heard them effectively answer is, "What caused this huge explosion, this 'Big Bang?'" After all, we know that nothing can be created from nothing. So, if that is true, then how does anything exist? I believe that herein rests our answer! If nothingness is the vast majority of what exists in the universe today, and if at one time the entire universe was nothingness, then what if the *natural* state of the universe is just nothingness? Most of the universe is empty space, from the stars in the sky to the pages of this book. Really, nothingness is far more common than anything else in the universe. So what if that's the case, what if the natural realm is *not* what we can see, taste, touch, smell, and hear? What if the natural world is undetectable because it is simply nothing?

For most of us, something supernatural is something that violates the very rules of existence, something outside the realm of nature. Well, if the true realm of nature is nothingness, then everything that exists would qualify as supernatural due to the fact that by merely existing it violates the realm of nature! If there was ever a time that the universe was completely void, empty of all things, then it would have taken a supernatural event just for a mere speck to exist. Every galaxy, star, and planet, every mountain, ocean, and rock, tree, plant, and animal would qualify as supernatural by the mere fact that none of these should exist to begin with.

Now let's take this a step further. Remember all those atoms we were talking about? Well, none of them are alive, not a single one. Yet somehow it is possible that a bunch of non-living particles can be assembled in such a way as to create a living being. That just doesn't make sense to me, a living creature composed entirely of non-living material. Non-living things can't suddenly be alive. If we were to see something that was not alive suddenly take on the characteristics of life, it would freak us out. Why? Because that would be something supernatural! The fact that all living creatures can be composed of non-living material is again nothing short of supernatural!

Maybe God isn't really hiding from us. Wouldn't it be just like us to miss Him while He is in plain view? Why do I need to see the mighty seas part when I can already look at a drop of water that shouldn't even exist? Why do I need to see a dead man rise when he shouldn't have ever been alive to begin with? Here we stand begging to experience the supernatural while we ourselves are the very evidence of the thing we are searching to see.

Perhaps the problem is not our inability to see the supernatural; rather, it's our inability to see what is natural. Perhaps the reason many of us claim to have never experienced the supernatural is not because we haven't; maybe it's because the supernatural is all we have ever experienced and, as a result, we have never noticed it. We must open our eyes and look around in absolute wonder. That lamp in the room, the carpet, the walls, the chair you are sitting on, the book you are reading, yes, even you, yourself, are supernatural!

2
What If God's Greatest Desire for Us Is Not Obedience?

In 1474, during the first international tribunal for war crimes, Peter von Hagenbach was on trial for a variety of crimes, including murder, rape, and perjury. In his defense von Hagenbach could only offer that he was simply following orders. This same defense was used again centuries later by several Nazi leaders regarding crimes of the Holocaust during the infamous Nuremberg Trials after World War II.

American social psychologist Stanley Milgram would discover with his Experiment on Obedience in 1961 that good and reasonable people can be capable of horrific acts when they are placed in a situation of simply following orders. The fact is, blind devotion can be a really good thing when the devotion is to a noble cause. But what about a cause that promotes evil and destruction? In this case, blind devotion could elicit horrific and negative consequences.

The problem is that if devotion truly is *blind* then one has no way of determining if they are following something good or bad. This condition is especially dangerous when something that is good gets warped by questionable ideologies. History shows us that blind devotion has led to monstrous acts where Christians were bound and burned at the stake by those who didn't share their beliefs. Strangely, having been victims of this type of tyranny, even Christians themselves have fallen prey to this dangerous mindset as shown through the atrocities committed during the crusades and inquisitions. Radical devotion has led religious fanatics to fly planes into buildings. It has resulted in extreme national pride that condones genocide.

What kind of devotion, strict obedience, and all out adherence to His laws does God require of us? Is radical compliance to the point of destruction the type of devotion God desires? Does He demand that His people dutifully follow orders without asking any questions?

These kinds of considerations force us to ask: What is God's greatest desire for humanity? Is it really just to obey Him? Or, instead, it is for us to be sinless? If we look at the words of Christ we may determine that God's greatest desire for us is to love our neighbors as ourselves, in addition to loving God with all of our heart, soul, strength, and mind. (Luke 10:27)

But do these actions really represent God's greatest desire for us? There was a time where I would have probably agreed that any of these things were God's greatest want for us. That suddenly changed once I realized I had the ability to *not* do any of the options list above.

For the most part, humanity has not always been very good at obeying God. We often fail to love our neighbor and we are often deficient at loving God. It is partly due to one's ability to refuse to love God or a neighbor that I now believe that obedience to Him does not represent God's greatest desire for us.

When you think about it, we really don't have to obey any of His commands! I have to believe that if God really wanted us to do these things, I mean really, really, wanted us to do them, then we would because we would have no choice. Yet, He doesn't *make* us obey His commands. Actually, He doesn't really *make* us do anything at all.

Therefore, I conclude that His desire for us *to have the ability not to obey Him* must be greater than His desire for us *to obey Him*. His desire for me *to have the ability to sin* must be greater than His desire for me *to be sinless*. His desire for me *to have the ability not to love my neighbor* and *not to love Him* must be greater than His desire for me *to love my neighbor or even to love Him*. I believe this because today these are freedoms I actually possess. Since I possess them, it can only be because He must want me to possess them.

In fact, one need look no further than the story of creation in Genesis to see that it is pretty clear that God actually *wants* us to have the *ability* to sin. Look at Genesis, Chapter 2. "And the Lord God made all kinds of trees grow out of the ground — trees that were pleasing to the eye and good for food. In the middle of the garden were the tree of life and the tree of the knowledge of good and evil… And the Lord God commanded the man, 'You are free to eat from any tree in the garden; but you must not eat from the tree of the knowledge of good and evil, for when you eat of it you will surely die.'" (Genesis 2:9, 16-17)

In this account of the creation of the universe man is given a paradise called the Garden of Eden in which to dwell. Within the boundaries of this garden God places a tree called the tree of the knowledge of good and evil. He commands Adam and Eve not to eat of the tree, but then leaves them with ample opportunity to do just that. In my opinion there is no clearer example in the Bible that God desired and meant for us to have the *ability* to sin.

Strange, isn't it? Why on earth would God actually desire

man to be able to sin? And if He really did want us to be able to sin then why would He ever have taken the time to come up with so many other rules? Shouldn't He have just left the rule book empty and let us do whatever we wanted?

What really happens to us when we break His rules? Many would say that He punishes us, but have you ever known someone who was struck by a lightning bolt right after they committed a sin? I have never heard of that actually happening to anyone. The truth is, I've committed plenty of sins in my life and not once has God struck me down. In fact, if I wanted to, I could put this computer down, get up, go out into the world and do unspeakable evils and God probably would not stop me. How do I know this? Because every day people around the world actually commit unspeakable evils and God doesn't stop them! Why?

Why doesn't God strike down the evil dictator before He attempts to annihilate an entire race of people? Why doesn't God halt the slave trader, or the man who kidnaps and enslaves young girls for a life of prostitution? Why doesn't God send the thunderbolt and strike down the sick and twisted individual who molests and murders innocent children? Clearly these acts are not within His will for us, but strangely, evil people still have the ability to commit these atrocities. I believe that their ability to commit horrific acts reveals God's greatest desire for man. Herein is freedom: the ability to sin.

One of the things that the Genesis creation account mentions about man is that he was created "in God's image." Therefore, many of God's characteristics have been shared with us as human beings. Perhaps God's absolute greatest characteristic is that He is a free creature. Nothing can contain Him, nothing can restrict Him, and nothing can stop Him. He is the perfect example of complete and total freedom. There is nothing He can't do, but there are many things He won't do.

If freedom is one of His characteristics He chose to share with us then the *ability* to sin was something He had to give us as well. After all, if man is not allowed to sin, then is he really free? How can I be truly free when there are things I'm not allowed to do?

The problem with this freedom is that it requires incredible responsibility for it to work properly. In fact, it is the very freedom God granted us that has ultimately led to our downfall. As a result of the freedom we possess, we have the power to encourage or oppress. We have the power to help or hurt. We have the power to love or hate.

When we look at the most tragic events in human history it seems that most of them were caused by people! I would wager to say that humans have done far more harm to each other than any series of natural disasters. Unbridled freedom can bring with it the potential for unbridled good, but unfortunately it can also result in unbridled evil and anarchy.

What if God is Like This?

Thus, the Bible was given as God's owner's manual to instruct us how to handle the freedom we possess. As I mentioned earlier, in order for man to truly be free man must possess the ability to sin. But what happens once we exercise that ability and cross the line into sin? Jesus tells us in John 8:34, "I tell you the truth, everyone who sins is a slave to sin." I think most of us would agree that anyone who is a slave is not someone who is free. So when we *do* sin we give up the freedom God granted us and willingly allow sin to become our master.

In order for man to be free we must possess the ability to sin, but we must not exercise that ability or we will lose the very freedom that having the ability to sin grants us. Some believe that Christ was sinless because he could not sin but I'm not sure that was the case. I believe He could have sinned if He had wanted to, but knowing that sinning would rob Him of freedom, He never did!

So, perhaps all these rules God gave us in the Bible weren't really rules at all. Perhaps they were instructions on how to preserve the freedom we have been given by Him.

God's instructions on how we are to live our lives, ultimately leaves us free to decide whether or not we want to adhere to His teachings. We have the freedom to choose to obey, or not.

Take the Ten Commandments, for instance. They are found

in Exodus, Chapter 20. In these God provides the Israelites ten basic rules for life. The first four deal directly with how we interact with God:

1. Don't have any gods ahead of God.
2. Don't worship idols.
3. Don't use God's name in vain.
4. Make sure you use the Sabbath to worship God.

The next six, though, were directed at how we are to treat each other. The fifth commandment states we are to honor our parents. But what happens to you or me when we fail to honor our parents? Does the earth open up and swallow us? Do flaming swords fly out of heaven and run us through? Not exactly. In fact, I'd bet that very few if any of us have ever experienced an undeniably supernatural consequence for disobeying this important command.

It might seem as if there are no consequences for violating this rule until you look at the natural results of ignoring it. Failing to honor our parents can lead to family strife, tensions, and fighting among those with whom we should be closest. A humorous observation I have made about this command, as a result of twelve years of youth ministry, is that kids, especially teenagers, tend not to like the idea of having to honor their parents. They will often ask the question, "What if I have bad parents?" Interestingly, ten years later these same teenagers have become extremely appreciative of the command to honor their father and mother once they become parents themselves.

Ultimately, failure to follow this command will lead to, or add to dysfunction and a lack of freedom within the family. The command is really for the child more than it is for the parent. But what about the case of a kid who parents are bad? A child can choose to live life imprisoned by bitterness and rage toward the parent, or the child can choose to honor the parent with something as simple as forgiveness. In that case, honoring the parent can free the child from the weight of those negative emotions and release the child from bitterness that often accompanies a lack of forgiveness.

God does not need to punish us for violating this command because violating it is its own punishment. The same can be said of the rest of the commandments. The person who engages in murder, adultery, thievery, coveting, or lying is a person God has no need to punish because the natural consequences of these activities will be their own punishment. The murderer will always be looking over his shoulder, fleeing the legal ramifications of his actions as well as the vengeance others want to inflict, not to mention the likelihood of mounting emotions of crushing guilt. The adulterous man will be trapped in a realm of secrecy and deceit along with the thief and the liar. The man who covets will be imprisoned in a world of envy, forever ungrateful with his own position in life, powerless to appreciate his blessings while he chooses to live devoted to the pursuit of things that never bring him fulfillment.

I'll never forget an incident involving a young man by the name of Alex. Alex was about fifteen years old when I met him. He had recently been arrested for possession of cocaine and was waiting for his juvenile court hearing. In the meantime, Alex's foster parents, Dave and Angie, were having a difficult time with him.

Alex's birth parents never married. He had not heard from his father in years and his mother was in prison on drug charges. Alex had been bounced around the foster care system and had landed for the last few years in the care of a wonderful Christian family that had a heart for the down and out. Alex failed to recognize how well he had it, though. He often snuck out and ran away, sometimes for days.

I first met Alex just before his arrest and assisted Dave and Angie in the process of getting him released. One of Alex's biggest obstacles to any chance of success was that his drug suppliers lived in his immediate neighborhood. Some even attended his school.

It was obvious to everyone who cared about Alex that he was rapidly reaching a dangerous point of no return on a path of self destruction. In a last ditch effort to try to save Alex from himself, Dave and Angie came to me and asked if I would be willing to talk to him about going to rehab. They had been successful in securing a bed for him at a rehab facility but were afraid he would run away if they forced him to go. They observed that I had developed a good rapport with Alex. They hoped that if I talked to him I might be able to convince him to attend rehab. I agreed to give it a try and told them I'd meet with him.

I swung by Alex's high school on the next day as classes were letting out, and noticed him walking alone toward an alley that led behind some houses. I pulled up next to him and called out my passenger window. Alex looked over with an astonished look on his face before giving me a sly grin and yelling out, "Hey man! What are you doing here?"

I told him I had come to pick him up to grab a bite to eat. Alex stopped for a second and looked into the alley where he was headed, then back at me. After a few moments of indecision he hopped in the car and said, "Alright, where we headed?"

We went down to a local fast food joint and ordered a couple of burgers, fries, and drinks before taking seats in one of the booths. I started off with some small talk about how his day at school was, but he only seemed half-interested. Alex then interrupted me mid-sentence and asked, "So did Dave and Angie put you up to this?" I was caught off-guard by his point-blank bluntness. Actually, I was pretty impressed by his insight.

"Well," I responded, trying to think of something to deflect the question, "Yeah, I guess…" It was not the quick-witted response I was hoping for. "But I would have done this anyway." Hmm, yeah, that sounded sincere… We're off to a good start now.

"Nice," he said. "Why don't you guys just leave me alone and let me live my life?"

"Are you enjoying your life?" I responded, now sensing that this plane was crashing before takeoff.

"Hell, yeah, I am!" he said.

Alex then went on to tell me about all the girls he was having sex with, how popular he had become among his friends, how he loved going to the parties, and how often and how much he could drink. He said he was frustrated by the restrictions of his foster parents and asked why they couldn't just trust him to take care of himself.

He reasoned, "I know what I'm doing, man. You're only a kid once, and I want to have fun before I turn eighteen and all this stuff stays on my permanent record."

During his entire rant I sat and quietly listened. (So far I was failing at talking anyway.)

Finally, during a lull, I asked him about his friends.

He shot back, "My friends got my back; they're there for me!"

What if God is Like This?

I asked him, "Where were they when you took the fall for all of them, accepting the blame for being in possession of cocaine when you guys were in the alley together?"

"I had to, they are all over eighteen; they would have been in way bigger trouble than me. I was doing what good friends do." He said.

"Were they there to pick you up when you were released?" I asked.

"They couldn't—they aren't my legal guardians."

"When you saw them again did they thank you?"

"They…." He stopped for a moment with his mouth open before continuing, "This is stupid!"

"Is it?" I asked, amping up my demeanor a bit.

I went further. "Alex, Dave and Angie have given you more than anybody in your life has ever given you. No matter how much you mess up they keep taking you back. Your friends wouldn't do that. If it benefitted them, they would turn on you in a second and you know that."

Alex sat and stared at his half-eaten burger with a blank expression on his face while swirling a fry in some ketchup.

I continued, "Alex, you keep talking about wanting to live your life, but so far, how is it working out for you? You're only fifteen and you've already been to jail. Plus, you are trapped in the prison of cocaine addiction."

That one must have hurt as he shot a momentary glare at me before looking back at his food, his eyes instantly swelling with tears.

"All these things you are talking about, the girls, the sex, the drugs, the parties, the drinking, none of it has added a single thing to your life, Alex. In fact, these things have robbed you of your life. Alex, I can't imagine having the upbringing you've had. I really can't. You have had to deal with more crap than any kid your age should, and that really can't be changed.

"When I was a kid, I grew up on a cattle ranch out in the middle of nowhere and my parents were pretty strict. I didn't have the opportunity to do all the things you talked about. You could say that I wasn't very 'free' if you wanted, but now I can see the opposite is true. I can see that due to my parent's restrictiveness I'm freer today than I would have been otherwise. I'm free from addiction. I'm free from the stupid decisions I would have made while high or drunk, and I'm free from the awkwardness that comes from crossing paths with old lovers. In fact, my freedom has even spilled over into the lives of others.

"My wife is free to know that there are no other women out there who have been with her husband." I was on a roll now. "Alex, freedom isn't about doing a bunch of stuff. Just because someone has experienced a lot doesn't mean that person has truly lived. Freedom is about where your decisions and choices lead you and what is left over afterward.

"I've found freedom in looking into the eyes of a man in Mexico after a group of us helped him build a house for his family. I've found it in the laughter of third world children as we fed them and played games with them. Freedom is more than just doing what feels good; it's bigger than us, Alex. It's bigger than getting high or going to a party."

Alex's face was now red and he was fighting hard to choke back the tears.

"Alex, some people find freedom in opening their home to a kid they don't know and loving him as if he was their own." That was the straw. Alex looked away from me and out a window as tears began streaming down his face.

We both sat in silence for a few moments while he tried to regain his composure.

"I've been so mean to them," he started with a quivering voice. "I've never believed anyone ever cared about me. I guess I didn't believe anyone ever would."

"I can definitely see how you would feel that way, Alex," I said. "But I think Dave and Angie have proven that they do."

After a few moments of silence I looked at Alex and told him I thought he needed to go to rehab. Alex stared at his plate with a blank look. After a few moments he began to slowly nod his head.

"Okay," he said, "I'll go. But not because I need it. I'll go to make them happy." I nodded and smiled.

When I dropped Alex off at home both Dave and Angie met him with hugs at the door. One of the more beautiful sights in my life was watching that family cry together.

I would later learn that Alex left the house again late that same night before they could go to rehab in the morning. He called them two days later and said that he was with his friends, that he was okay. He said he was certain that he could beat his addiction on his own, without rehab, and didn't want to be forced into something he didn't need.

That's the thing about sin: It is a prison of the mind as much as it is a prison of the body. Even when freedom seems within reach it still has the power to hold one captive.

God really has no need to punish people for sin as they are subjecting themselves to their very own hells. It's kind of like a parent telling a child not to touch the hot stove. If the child decides to disobey and touch the hot stove anyway, the parent would not need to spank the child. The blistering skin and accompanying pain would be the child's punishments for disobedience.

What if God's rules are like this? What if they really aren't rules at all? Instead, what if they are warnings for us, warnings not to engage in certain activities that cause injury, so we won't be robbed of our freedom?

A dear friend of mine who is a Byzantine priest made the observation during a conversation we once had, that God's moral laws are similar to the physical laws that govern the universe. One cannot *break* the commandment not to lie any more than one can *break* the law of gravity. When anyone attempts to break the law of gravity the only thing that gets broken is that person. The same is true for every other command. When we attempt to break God's moral laws, all that is accomplished is the shattering of our own lives. If this is the case then God is not subjecting any of us to some sort of strange ethics test; instead, He is giving us the tools we need to experience the best of life, a free life reserved only for Himself and the creature He created in His image, a life that is "to the full." (John 10:10)   We choose how to use His tools.

This is an area where religion can and really should look to God for guidance. God has given us instructions, advising us what is best to do and not to do, but then He stops there, leaving us the freedom to make our own decisions and choices in the matter. The church, on the other hand, has had a history of not only telling people how to live their lives, but trying to enforce its dictates as well! In extreme cases these impositions have led to inquisitions in which people have been tortured and killed for failing to obey. In lesser cases this takes the form of churches telling their congregants they can't drink, smoke, chew tobacco, go dancing, or attend movies. Either way, these legalistic rules have resulted in churches trying to control their people.

Control like this robs man of the freedom to sin which, ironically, robs him of his freedom altogether, negating the very intention God had for man to begin with. What a shame that religion itself could actually become an obstacle for mankind, standing in the way of the very freedom God is so intent on us possessing.

3
The Result of Freedom

The first chapter of Genesis begins by describing that God existed in a void of empty space. Over the course of six "days" He creates the sun, moon, stars, oceans, land, plants, and animals. Not bad for six day's work! I'll bet He worked some overtime in there somewhere. Finally on the last "day" He goes for the grand finale, the pinnacle of His creation. He creates the only creature that will exist in His image, the human being. It's the cherry on top, if you will.

At the conclusion of the whole process God surveys His sprawling creation. The stars are shining, galaxies are swirling, and planets are in orbit. As He gazes upon His magnificent universe everything looks good from His vantage point, so He zooms in on one particular galaxy that we have since named the Milky Way. Within that expansive Milky Way galaxy, He zeros in even closer to a very average star we call the sun. Orbiting around the sun is a fascinating little jewel of a planet called Earth.

God continues to dive further into the creation and targets a utopian paradise called the Garden of Eden, a place He created in which man will dwell. Here the birds are chirping, bunnies are hopping, and flowers are blooming while the deer and the antelope play. God's voice then booms throughout the universe as He declares, "It is good."

As with most things in life this garden comes with some instructions. Man can't just go out running willy-nilly in this thing. You see, within this garden, at the very center, two rather unique trees are planted and growing. From one tree, the tree of life, man is told he may eat the fruit freely. The other tree, referenced in Chapter 1, is called the tree of the knowledge of good and evil. Man is strictly warned not to eat any fruit from it. In fact, man is even warned he will die should he decide to eat the fruit from this thing.

For years I found the existence of this tree to be a little baffling. If we were not supposed to eat of this tree, why would God make it to begin with? Well, as was mentioned earlier, one of the things that we need, to truly be free, is the ability to sin. The existence of this tree fulfilled this purpose for us. Its existence granted us the ability to sin.

Unfortunately as much as this tree provided freedom for us, it also provided our avenue to lose it. To make matters worse, we were told that if we ate it we would die as well! Not good.

God basically created a way for us to kill ourselves! Why would He do that? I would think that not having the freedom to sin would still be better than death! Imagine bringing a loaded gun into a nursery full of children and placing it with the toys, then telling the kids they can play with all the toys except the black one with the shiny handle! It makes no sense! What purpose could the freedom granted by this tree possibly have had that would justify such a huge risk? After wondering about this for much of my life, a possible answer finally began to present itself. It did so after I became a parent.

Let's go back to our story for a second. After God completed the creation of the universe He declared it to be good, and this good universe included the tree of the knowledge of good and evil. I decided to give God the benefit of the doubt here in that if He declared the universe to be good, and the universe contained the tree of knowledge of good and evil, then without the tree of the knowledge of good and evil the universe would not have been good. We must conclude then that this tree obviously had some purpose in the universe. I just didn't know what it was—kind of like the mosquito.

When I became a parent, my entire world changed. I suddenly was introduced to a type of love I hadn't known existed. Never before had I experienced a love that was more powerful, tender, reaching, or innocent. For the first time in my life, I loved someone completely and totally unconditionally, knowing that person could do nothing to earn my love in return.

Even the love of a spouse is different than this, in that when a couple meets there are so many different factors that dictate first attraction. A person's looks, personality, likes, and dislikes all play a roll in how we come to choose a person as a spouse. But with children, none of those things matter. You just love them. It is really quite beautiful as the children never fully understand a parent's love for them until they become parents themselves.

Now I think I speak for many parents when I share at least one fleeting fear: the fear that your child won't love you back. If you are a parent, how many times have you listened to your child yell out in a tantrum, "I hate you!" After a brief chuckle due to the child's antics, you secretly worry that perhaps your child really does hate you! You then quickly return to your senses and think, "That's crazy talk. Of course she doesn't hate me… At least I don't think she does…" It is the natural desire for every parent that their child love them back even if it is only a fraction of the amount of love that the parent feels for them.

Now, why would God be any different than this? After all, God is a parent, too. Just like a daughter can't fully understand the magnitude of love her parents have for her, perhaps we can't fully understand the magnitude of the love God has for us. Wouldn't it be natural for the God who loves us so immensely, to desire our love in return or at least desire that we have the opportunity to love Him in return even if we can only give Him a fraction of the amount of love He feels for us?

Perhaps this was the reason for that darn tree. Perhaps this was the reason for our freedom. Think about it: the only way for someone to truly love another person is to have the ability *not to love them.* To have the ability not to love someone requires *freedom*!

One of the great beauties of true love is the fact that it doesn't have to be given. Love is just as much a choice as it is a feeling, maybe more so. What makes my wife's love for me so special is that there are millions of other guys out there in this world she could have loved, but for some reason she chose me. (Okay, it's obvious why she chose me, but that's not the point.) I treasure her love because she didn't have to give it to me. The very fact that she didn't have to give it to me is the very thing that makes it so special.

Love is only valid where free will exists. If one can't choose to love, one can't love. Had God simply created man to live in the garden without providing an avenue to love Him back then man would have simply been a robot with no independent choice, no freedom, no ability to love, and no ability not to love.

Maybe by creating that tree God gave us the other option. What if He was actually granting us true freedom by creating a way for us not to love Him, and by doing so, actually instilled in us the ability to do just the opposite, to love Him back! With the creation of that tree, God set us apart from every other creature that was ever made. He gave us a choice that was uniquely ours: the choice to disobey Him or, depending on how you look at it, the choice to *obey* Him. Ultimately, He gave man the freedom to love his creator.

It should be noted though: I still don't know why the mosquito is here.

4
What If God Is Dealing with a Personal Crisis?

What a beautiful scene we have now: a wondrously vast universe that contains the treasured planet Earth, and on that planet man and God interacting lovingly in the Garden of Eden like a father with his children. Boy, anything this good has to have a great ending, right? After all, what could possibly go wrong? Let's read the rest of this happy story.

"Now the serpent was more crafty than any of the wild animals the Lord God had made. He said to woman, 'Did God really say, "You must not eat from any tree in the garden?"' The woman said to the serpent, 'We may eat fruit from the trees in the garden, but God did say, "You must not eat fruit from the tree that is in the middle of the garden, and you must not touch it, or you will die."' 'You will not surely die,' the serpent said to the woman. 'For God knows that when you eat of it your eyes will be opened, and you will be like God, knowing good and evil.'

"When the woman saw that the fruit of the tree was good for food and pleasing to the eye, and also desirable for gaining wisdom, she took some and ate it. She also gave some to her husband, who was with her, and he ate it. Then the eyes of both of them were opened, and they realized they were naked, so they sewed fig leaves together and made coverings for themselves.

"Then the man and his wife heard the sound of the Lord God as he was walking in the garden in the cool of the day, and they hid from the Lord God among the trees of the garden. But the Lord God called to the man, 'Where are you?' He answered, 'I heard you in the garden, and I was afraid because I was naked, so I hid.' And he said, 'Who told you that you were naked? Have you eaten from the tree that I commanded you not to eat from?' The man said, 'The woman you put here with me — she gave me some fruit from the tree, and I ate it.' (Genesis 3:1-12)

What!? Are you kidding me?! I mean, come on, a talking snake? Shouldn't there have been something somewhat

What if God is Like This?

suspicious about this? This is where we can really see Eve suffering greatly from not having a mother. If this had been you or me, you know we all would have remembered our mother's voice in our heads warning, "Stranger! Danger! Stranger! Danger! Don't ever talk to strangers!" I can't tell you how many times I have had some sort of reptile come up to me and start making suggestions, but thanks to my mother's advice, I immediately decided against whatever it was telling me to do. Nothing good can come from a talking snake. Honestly, anytime I turn on the TV and find a talking animal promoting a product I immediately become suspicious.

I'd be willing to bet that since Eve was the very first mother she is probably the source of our "Stranger! Danger!" warnings. I imagine her later in life taking her two young boys, Cain and Abel, into her lap (before they hated each other), and giving them this sound instruction: "Now listen boys, as you know I'm the very first mommy the world has ever known, so I'm kind of learning this on the fly, but I have my first bit of motherly wisdom I'd like to share with you two."

"Sure mom, what is it?"

"Don't talk to strangers."

"Well, okay, Mom, but why is that?"

"Just trust me on this one."

Adam, on the other hand, picks up on being a husband much faster. His sense of self-defense immediately kicked in when God showed up and he had the wherewithal to at least blame his wife. That was quick thinking. In fact, he not only blamed his wife, he even blamed God! "The woman that *You* gave me..." I have found that blaming God is typically a good strategy when dodging any responsibility for sin.

Okay, all kidding aside, I'm guessing for most of you this was not exactly the surprise ending that it was for me. With this one bad decision, man encounters some pretty hefty penalties. Man is separated from God and doomed to an eternity without Him. The garden, paradise, freedom, all of it, is now lost. This sounds like humankind has got a real problem! There are few feelings worse than the feeling of not being free. But one feeling that competes with it is the feeling of being lost.

This is especially true for children. When I was about ten years old, my parents took our family to Hawaii on vacation. One night we decided to walk from our hotel in downtown Honolulu to find a place to eat. As we were walking down the street, I began to ask my father a question. About midway through my question I looked up at him to get his response only to realize the man walking next to me was not my father! I stopped for a moment and looked in every direction. My family was nowhere to be found. Ahead of me was only a sidewalk occupied solely by the man who had just been walking next to me, now continuing on his way. My young mind raced as I quickly began preparing myself for the possibility of living out the rest of my days as an orphaned Hawaiian street urchin, which, looking back on it now might not have been too bad!

I could already imagine my family on the airplane heading back home wondering what happened to me. I figured it was only a matter of time before my face would appear on milk cartons and billboards. I started walking back down the sidewalk in the direction I had come from and approached an intersection. When I looked to my left, I saw an extremely busy street, bustling with patrons of the downtown night life, each of which I was sure was a child predator just waiting to kidnap me. I remember looking around and thinking, "This must have been the direction my family had turned" as I could see a good distance down the streets in every other direction.

By this time I was terrified and began desperately looking for a police officer but, of course, there were none. Those guys are never around when you need them. I really didn't want to venture down the sidewalk into the crowd of people but I reasoned that this was the only possible direction I could go.

I took a gulp and slowly stepped into the mass of humanity, certain that the boogie man was just crouching, ready to snatch me up in the crowd. As I started into the forest of waistlines and torsos, I locked on to the only set of eyes at my level. They belonged to a boy about my age who was walking with his mother. I approached him and began trying to describe my family to him, hoping he had seen them pass. Just as he was about to answer me, I heard a familiar voice frantically calling my name. I gazed farther into the crowd but didn't see anything. Then suddenly my mother emerged, shoving people aside, followed closely by my brother. She took hold of my arm, letting out a frantic sigh of relief, and put to an end my terrifying ordeal. For many years after this I was convinced that the feeling of being lost was the worst emotion a person could experience.

Seventeen years would pass before I would learn there is actually desperation even more terrifying than being a lost child. It was the feeling my mother experienced that night in Honolulu, the feeling suffered by the *parent* of a lost child. Ironically this experience would take place on a vacation as well—so much for relaxing.

One summer I took my family to sunny San Diego to get some rest and spend some time away from the daily grind. My oldest son was three at the time and we headed to Mission Beach for the 4th of July. If you have been there you know that beach is bustling and crowded that time of year. Wanting to enjoy our time in the sun, we staked our claim to a small portion of sand near one of the lifeguard shacks and began to relax.

We were vacationing with some dear friends of ours so

What if God is Like This?

there were plenty of eyes to help monitor the kids. I pointed out the bright red flag on the lifeguard shack and told my son that if he were to somehow get lost (like *that* would ever happen) to go to the red flag. Sure enough, about two hours later, my wife asked that sickening question, "Hey, where's William?!" Having just checked on him about a minute before, I calmly scanned the children in our group and noticed that one was missing. Of course that one wasn't any kid, it was *my* kid — at the time my only kid.

I jumped up nervously and looked over at the red flag, but there were no toddlers anywhere in sight. Next, in a moment of horror, I feared he could have walked down to the water and been swept away. Logic then kicked in for a moment and I remembered he was afraid of the water and had refused to go near it all day. The adults in our group split up, half of us heading south while the others ventured north.

Frantic thoughts raced through my mind at this point and I began to worry I had seen my son for the last time. Seconds seem like hours. I feared the worst. I ran down the beach about a hundred yards. Thinking he could not have made it that far yet, I turned around, and slowly began walking back, checking every person on the way. Then, I heard my wife yell, "There he is!" I looked up and saw my wife running up the beach and past her was our son in his neon green swimsuit, holding the hand of a woman and leading her back to the red flag.

I remember feeling so incredibly grateful to this wonderful lady as there was no way to repay her for what she had done. I was ready to go to any length to get my son back and would have stopped at nothing until he was safely in my arms.

I can barely imagine the horror that parents who have lost their children or whose children have been abducted must go through. It honestly has to be the worst kind of torment one can experience. And it's a horror that God Himself knows personally, for He was feeling it that day in the garden.

God had a real problem! Once that fruit was consumed He had lost His children. As mentioned earlier, He loved His creation in ways that man will never fully understand. To keep things in perspective, imagine a parent telling a child not to wander outside the fenced backyard while playing. If the child were to disobey and become lost, only a deranged parent would say, "Oh well, serves him right, I told him not to leave the yard." We all know a real parent's immediate concern would be to locate their child and go to any length to find and save that child. Would God act any differently?

Take a look at God's immediate response to the situation. The first thing He said to Adam was, "Where are you?" Isn't that a strange question for an all-knowing God to ask? Of course He knew Adam was hiding behind the third bush on the left, but He still asked the question.

The very nature of this question implied separation. You

don't ask someone where they are when you are standing right there with them. You ask this question when they are apart from you.

God immediately knew something was wrong. He could feel the separation that had taken place between Himself and His children. They used to walk happily in the garden together, but now something had changed. A division was present, the man and woman were not there, their spirits could not intertwine with His like they used to. He knew His kids were missing and He didn't like it. And like any good parent, He stopped at nothing. He began the relentless pursuit to bring them back with no regard to the cost or sacrifice.

5
What If Hell Wasn't Created for People?

I was ordained as a pastor in Las Vegas, Nevada. This may explain a lot of things for some of you. Perhaps the only thing less credible would be if I had received my ordination over the Internet which, to be honest, was quite the temptation on those nights I was up till 2:00 AM trying to complete a paper due the next day.

My church denomination holds an annual meeting where the latest crop of new pastors receives their ordination credentials. The meeting takes place in different areas of the Southwest, and this time it was Sin City's turn to host us.

Will Hathaway

I will never forget that after the ceremony a few of us headed down to The Strip to get dinner. Yes, it was only to get dinner. I was filled with the satisfaction that I was now a fully ordained minister as we walked in front of the casinos on Las Vegas Boulevard. I joked with my wife and the couple we were with about paying for our trip to Vegas by performing a few weddings. Right about then I heard a monstrous voice, "You're going to burn in Hell!" Startled, I stopped and thought, "Wow, well, okay, maybe I won't perform any weddings. It was just a joke."

I looked toward the street corner and before me was a man standing on a box, yelling out to the mingling crowds, "You are all going to burn in an eternal Hell!" What a spectacle he was. It was interesting that the crowds just walked right past this guy like he wasn't even there, almost like he was a regular or something. His message and method were so common and out of place that he wasn't even heard.

I remember feeling ill at this guy's tactics for "reaching" people. I also became acutely aware that as an official minister I was now linked with fanatics like this in the minds of many. Every time he yelled out to the crowd he made their fiery futures very clear, and what troubled me most was that he didn't even seem to have any concern or compassion in his voice. His was a pronouncement of judgment, not an encouragement toward God. His message was condemnation,

What if God is Like This?

not care; it was criticism, not compassion.

I wanted to run up to this guy and tell him to shut up. I wanted to tell him his messages and methods were revolting and crude, and he was influencing no one in the right way.

As I considered how I would put him in his place, I thought better about it and decided to leave him alone. It was then that the teachings I had received all those years flooded in. The memories were troubling as I was reminded that the Bible really does talk about Hell a lot, in fact far too much for my comfort level. For a long time the topic of Hell had bothered me greatly. To be honest, it had never made any sense to me. Thanks to that sappy soap box preacher all the conflicts about Hell re-flooded my mind.

Come on, don't you ever wonder why the consequence of any sin has to be an eternity languishing in Hell? As a youth pastor I often had kids ask me how a good God could sentence people to an eternity in Hell. Inwardly I had to admit that I really hated that question, mainly because it is a good one.

Think about this. Two people eat fruit off a tree that they are not supposed to eat and *boom!* the punishment is eternal torment?! It's torment not only for them but for every single person ever to be born after them?! That hardly seems fair! In fact, it actually seems sadistic, tyrannical, and cruel!

How can Christians call their God *loving* when this eternal torment for a single offense is the design He created? After all, this is basically like a parent walking into the kitchen as their child is taking a cookie out of the cookie jar and immediately punishing the child and all his descendants with lifetimes of unremitting torture! Talk about the punishment not fitting the crime! How could God do such a thing?

Well, my experience with the Bible has shown me that when something doesn't make sense there is typically a whole lot more to the story. I mean, really, if we as mere humans are smart enough to look at something and see it as an injustice, then shouldn't we understand that God sees injustice as well? We may not get every one of life's answers from the Bible, but I think there are enough answers there that we can trust God with some of the ones that aren't.

There are some things we just have to leave in the hands of God and be at peace with the idea that perhaps we don't have all the information. Honestly, does the God of the universe really owe us any explanations?

Fortunately, when it comes to our questions about Hell, the Bible does present very clear answers. I had to learn them.

The more I studied the concept of Hell in scripture, the more this terrible place seemed to make some sense. As I learned more about the reasons for the existence of this troubling realm I began to see the level of desperation God displayed to keep us from ever experiencing it.

I want to express a bit of frustration on the topic of Hell. I

What if God is Like This?

think Hell is a concept that Christians have misused. It has been employed as a fear tactic to scare people into Christianity and in some instances it's been engaged as a method of coercing people into submission to oppressive ideologies. What better way to keep people in line than for their religious leaders to tell them they are going to Hell unless they act in certain ways and believe in certain things?

What a great way to rob people of their God-given freedom. Generations of preachers have stood behind pulpits and on street corners telling people that they are going to burn in the fires of Hell if they refuse to accept Jesus as their Lord and Savior. Many of these preachers may have had good intentions, which is ironic because we all know which road is paved with good intentions, but the true message of Christianity has never been "Accept Christ or go to Hell." When it's been presented that way, I believe we have misrepresented Christ and, as a result, engaged in nothing short of sin! I believe many more people have been driven away from Christ through this method of sharing God's love than were ever drawn to Him through it.

That said I want to explore this extreme consequence of sin. Whether we like it or not (hopefully not), the Bible acknowledges the presence of Hell. Because it exists we have to deal with the difficult question as to why God would create such a horrible place as a consequence for what appeared to be a relatively small sin. The Bible actually holds the answers to these questions. The problem is that many of our church clergy and friendly street preachers don't turn to these passages enough to ensure what they are saying is Biblically true.

One of my favorite scriptures about Hell, if such a thing can be termed "favorite," is Matthew 25:41-43. Here Jesus is describing God's judgment and states, "Then he will say to those on his left, 'Depart from me, you who are cursed, into the eternal fire *prepared for the devil and his angels.* For I was thirsty and you gave me nothing to drink, I was a stranger and you did not invite me in, I needed clothes and you did not clothe me, I was sick and in prison and you did not look after me.'"

There now. Isn't that a pleasant passage? It just gives me warm fuzzies all over every time I read it. No, seriously, did you catch what it said? There was actually a very interesting piece of information Jesus gave us there! He said, "Depart from me, you who are cursed, into the eternal fire prepared for the devil and his angels." You see, Hell was made for the devil and his angels. Hell was *not* made for us! That's an important technicality because it tells us why Hell even exists.

Think about how much that truth changes the context of Hell as far as it relates to mankind. It was never meant as a place for us to inhabit! It was designed as the destiny for the greatest evildoer ever to exist, the vilest of the vile, the very devil himself and his terrible demons. They were the only ones God had in mind when He created this place. Now if you look at Hell from the perspective that the criminal meant to inhabit it was Satan, suddenly the punishment seems to match the crime a little more.

So what went wrong? What happened, that man can be sucked into this realm of torment?

"Everyone who sins breaks the law. In fact, sin is lawlessness. But you know that Jesus appeared so that he might take away our sin. And in him is no sin." (I John 3:4-5)

This is a key passage. It explains how God and sin interact: they don't. Christ and sin do not dwell together. Since Christ was the Son of God then I think we are pretty safe to say that there is also no sin in God, either. If God can't dwell with sin, then that means sin would have to exist somewhere outside of His presence, right? That would explain passages like these (italics added):

"I say to you that many will come from the east and the west, and will take their places at the feast with Abraham, Isaac, and Jacob in the kingdom of heaven. But the subjects of the kingdom will be thrown *outside*, into the darkness, where there will be weeping and gnashing of teeth." (Matthew 8:11-12)

"Then the king told the attendants, 'Tie him hand and foot, and throw him *outside*, into the darkness, where there will be weeping and gnashing of teeth.'" (Matthew 8:13)

"Then they will *go away* to eternal punishment, but the righteous to eternal life." (Matthew 25:46)

"There will be weeping there, and gnashing of teeth, when you see Abraham, Isaac and Jacob and all the prophets in the kingdom of God, but you yourselves *thrown out*." (Luke 13:28)

The list could go on, but I think the point is made. This is a recurring theme. It is that those who are bound for Hell *are not in God's presence*. They are somewhere else, somewhere away from Him.

Sin, by its very nature, is an imperfection. So if God is perfect, then how could imperfection co-exist with perfection? They are oil and water; they can't mix. It would be as if God were a one million gallon tank of pure water and a human was a thimble full of muddy water. If that thimble, as small as it is, were to be poured into that million gallon tank then the entire tank would be tainted.

Essentially, God had to create a place for sin to dwell that was outside of His presence. One of God's characteristics is His omnipresence, meaning He is in all places all of the time, which of course makes it kind of hard to get away from Him. It's almost like God had to take an area and pull all of His Spirit out of it—a God vacuum if you will.

I believe this is what Hell is. It is simply a Godless place, the only place where God doesn't exist, a place completely

What if God is Like This?

void of Him, a state of existence originally designed for Satan and his demons. Since God and sin cannot coexist, and since man became sinful in the Garden of Eden, there is nowhere else for sinful man to dwell other than this place where God does not.

This might well explain why a man would go to Hell but it doesn't explain why Hell had to be such a horrible, tormenting realm. After all, did God really have to make it such a painful and terrible dwelling place? If He loves man so much, why would He ever send him to a place like this? Why couldn't He have left Hell for Satan and just created a static room with white walls, no furniture, and re-runs of soap operas for man to occupy outside His presence?

Let me propose a theory regarding that idea. What exactly would a place that is completely void of God's presence look like? If God is the source of all joy, all happiness, all hope, all love, light, peace, and comfort, if He is the source of all that is good, then what would the characteristics be of a place without Him? Wouldn't this dimension be a lonely, dark, hopeless place, where love, peace, and comfort do not exist? Could you possibly think of a more horrible realm than one where God is not present in any form?

I don't think God sat up in heaven with a big smile and a cynical laugh straining on the very bellows that fan the fires of Hell. I don't think He even had to try to make it a bad place. I think Hell is all that is left when God completely removes Himself from any situation. Its terrors are the natural results of His absence, not the results of deliberate and concentrated desires to inflict torture.

Think about the punishment given to the worst criminals in our society. They receive the dreaded solitary confinement, hours and days on end with nobody to talk to, nobody to look at, no interaction with another human being. Really, the torment of solitary confinement is more about what is not there rather than what is.

The same application is used when parents put their kids in a "time out." A child is made to sit outside the presence of others for awhile. It is the aloneness that creates the punishment, the inability to receive attention or engage in any wanted activity.

Hell is really the ultimate "time out." Its horrors and torments are not created by what is there, but rather by what is not there. It is because God isn't there that it truly becomes a reality so bad that things just can't get any worse. This is a place from which God desperately wants to rescue us.

6
What If Some Things Are Hard for God?

A further examination of the fateful scene in the Garden of Eden that led to the loss of man's freedom leads me to admit that a lot of emotion is lost when we simply read the words. There is no emotion or inflection on the printed pages that capture God's mood as He asks Adam to reveal himself.

As a parent I read and weigh those words very differently than I did as a child, or even growing up. Now I hear a different tone when I review God's questions to Adam. I become keenly aware of a sense of desperation as God calls out to Adam and Eve, "Where are you?"

I wonder: if we had been there to hear God in person would we not have heard the same tone in His voice as that of the parent who had lost their child, the tone I heard in my mother's voice as she called my name in the crowd, and the tones of my wife and I searching for our son on the beach?

God knows the full effects of sin. He knows the consequences of being outside His presence. At the same time He risks giving man the opportunity to become sinful, a risk He determined to be reasonable in order for us to gain the experience of freedom and the ability to love.

So now what? What does God do? Well, He does what any good parent would do. He goes after His kid! He immediately mounts His efforts to rescue mankind and sets in motion the relentless processes of bringing about our redemption, processes that I believe pushed Him to His very limits as an omnipotent being. It was a stage that took several thousand years to set, but when the timing was right, He took the form of a man in His quest to "…seek and to save what was lost." (Luke 19:10)

Some readers may struggle with this concept, particularly if their father abandoned them, ignored them, or emotionally wounded them. It might be hard to imagine what a truly loving and caring father would be like, the kind of father who would defend, pursue, and let the child know they were worth loving and saving at any cost. As hard as it might be for an abandoned or abused child to imagine, this is the kind of father God really is. This is truly His character.

One of my most memorable encounters as a youth pastor involved someone who was not in my youth group. Her name was Megan. She was a young lady of twenty years with a mind full of questions about God. I had developed a friendship with her when she began attending our church about the same time I was hired. She had practically been adopted by the family of a girl in our youth group and had become a regular around the church.

After several months, she asked me if I could meet with her to discuss some of her questions about Christ and Christianity. We met in my office and I remember we conversed a little over an hour as she shared her story with me. She revealed some painful experiences in her life, including a couple of significant betrayals.

In response to her questions, I shared with her the story of Christ from Genesis to Jesus. At one point, she began sobbing as I told her about the cross. There were a few moments of silent sobbing as I related the magnitude of the sacrifice of Jesus.

A few moments passed and I asked her, "Because of the past betrayals in your life, could you be afraid that the story of Jesus wasn't true and therefore might simply be one more disappointment, one more betrayal waiting to happen?" She shocked me by responding, "No. No, actually I'm more afraid that it is true, that God really did go through so much for me." Moved by this honesty, I prayed for her and our meeting concluded. About two days later she informed me she had indeed committed her life to Christ.

In this chapter I'm going to cover some characteristics about God that, like Megan, I'm afraid might be true. I am going to share some ideas about the cross that I personally have not heard talked about in any churches. I'm not saying they aren't out there, I just have not found them anywhere. Please understand that these are *what if* type ideas about God.

I have come to believe that the Cross of Christ may have been much bigger and more terrible than I ever imagined. I think this truth is important because it also has to mean that God's love is also much bigger and more amazing than I ever dreamed.

One of the natural results of man trying to understand an omnipotent God is that different aspects of His existence may have to be diluted in order for us to wrap our minds around even part of the immensity of God. Essentially by breaking things down into concepts we can grasp, we can reduce or water down the very truths we are trying to understand.

One area where I think this has happened is in the concept of the cross. How can we possibly ever fully wrap our minds around the idea of God sacrificing Himself to purchase our salvation? Any attempt of any man to explain this phenomenon will fall far short of the reality of the event and its true meaning. I don't know if anybody else has ever felt this way, but I have spent a good portion of my life struggling with the magnitude of the cross: the necessity for it, the idea that it was hard for God, and how I am to respond to it.

Growing up in a Christian home, I understood the cross was something special, but mostly it was an event I learned to feel guilty about. The impression I had was that I had been bad and because of that, Jesus had to die on the cross. If guilt was the ultimate goal, I have to admit it worked pretty well on me.

I'm ashamed to admit this, but for a long time I never really saw the cross as something more than a grand inconvenience for God. I mean really, He is The Being of Unlimited Power. Can anything truly be hard for Him? When presented with a problem, shouldn't He be able to just draw on more and more of that power until He can overwhelm whatever issue arises? I understood Christ died, but was it really like He died and experienced real death when He was back among the living three days later, especially since He even knew He would be back in three days? This wasn't like a normal person dying, resulting in permanent loss. This was, although painful, a temporary problem for God that both He and Jesus knew would be over soon.

This may sound blasphemous, but I think more people would be willing to pay the ultimate price for something if they could be assured they would be alive again in three days. How could this really be such a huge sacrifice for Christ? I really felt like I was missing something in my limited understanding. I felt that there had to be more to this mysterious story about the price God paid for my soul.

The more I studied the cross, the more I gathered conflicting information. Logic told me that due to God's power the cross shouldn't have been all that bad for Him. But everything the Bible describes about the cross indicates just the opposite: that the cross was something extremely hard for Christ, the most difficult challenge He ever faced.

One needs to look no farther than the Garden of Gethsemane to see this. Jesus, God in the flesh, was literally brought to His knees and reduced to begging, of all things, for an easier way! What are we dealing with here? What kind of an event is so daunting that it has the power to bring the very Christ to his knees?

When you read the gospel accounts you can see the man is a complete train-wreck, sweating drops of blood, lonely, crying, praying, and pleading with his friends to stay awake with Him. What's going on here? These are by no means the actions of one who is about to take on an easy task, or even a mildly challenging one for that matter. What kind of an event

What if God is Like This?

would have this kind of effect on an omnipotent being?

All of this leads me to believe that the cross must have been far larger and more significant than I ever understood it to be. This cross was much more than, "You were a bad boy when you were little and now I have to do this." I believe this was a responsibility so big that it took every ounce of power from a being whose power is limitless.

I am going to present a theory about the cross and God's interaction with it. In August of 2008 I presented a sermon in which I sought to illustrate that God is not bound by the conventions of time as we understand them, the minutes, hours, days, and years. The basis for my illustration originated from Peter's second letter: "But do not forget this one thing, dear friends: With the Lord a day is like a thousand years, and a thousand years are like a day." (2 Peter 3:8) This verse clearly shows us that God does not interact with time in the same ways that we do.

Imagine you walk into a great museum and venture down one of its long hallways. On one of the walls a mural is hung that stretches the entire length of this hall. You look to the far left of the mural and begin to move your eyes slowly to the right. You see images depicted from the very beginning of time: the creation of the universe, Adam and Eve and their fateful encounter with the serpent, the building of the pyramids in Egypt and South America, the Israelites crossing the Red Sea. You witness the rise and fall of ancient empires. You see Jesus and His disciples, the Ascension, the upper room, then the travels, preaching, and teaching of the Apostle Paul. You see the fall of Rome, the Dark Ages, the Renaissance, the discovery of the Americas. You see everything up to and including your era. At one point you even see yourself, your entire life. As you move your eyes to the far right you view the Apocalypse, the end of the world, and the end of time. From your position you are able to view all of time all at once simply by gazing upon this mural.

Time has no meaning—you are outside the mural. Concepts of "before" and "after" only relate to those trapped inside the painting, not you. If you choose you can witness the same moment over and over again, or you can bounce around from future to past to future again. There are no limits to your access to any era, event, or moment. There are no questions as to what's next because every situation is in your line of sight.

Herein is a vague description of how God might see the universe. He stands firmly outside of the constructs of time, examining everything all at once without end. No moment escapes Him because He has access to every single one of them. Time never comes, it never goes. For God the moment is always right now, no matter what moment that is.

Somewhere on that painting the cross of Christ is fearlessly depicted. Boldly sketched there on the mural hanging on this immense wall is every moment of agony and torment of the events of the cross, from the Garden of Gethsemane to the Resurrection, the betrayal, the thorny crown, the lies and accusations, the torture, the walk to Golgatha, the whole thing is portrayed right there. It is neither coming nor going, it just is. It's just there, always, never ending, forever present, punctuating that mural.

Our understanding is that the cross composed a three day event. But being outside of time, what was the cross for God? What if the cross was and is constantly in front of God the Father? What if it is an event He always bears? What if, from God's perspective, the cross is forever before Him?

Remember, the result of sin is eternal separation from God. So wouldn't it make sense that perhaps Jesus paid an eternal, everlasting price? What if there is a part of Christ that, from God's perspective, is and always will be, on that cross? If this is the case then the cross is a point of torment that will never end, even for an all-powerful God. In fact, it would take an eternally all-powerful being to even endure it.

My heart breaks at the possibility that God would do so much for me, and for you, and for us all. Though I'm somewhat afraid to share it with you, I think there is still more to this terrible price that God paid.

The full effects of the mystery of the cross are something man may never fully grasp, but I think we can get a glimpse of the magnitude of what is happening by watching and listening to Jesus' own words as He experiences this horrible ordeal. At one point Jesus cries out from the cross in anguish, "My God, my God, why have you forsaken me?" (Matthew 27:46) What does this haunting cry reveal to us? Remember how sin causes separation from God? I think we can determine at this point that Jesus is experiencing full and complete separation from God.

Let's just think about this for a moment. Jesus *was* God and He is now experiencing *separation* from God. I believe this is another reason the cross was such a horrific experience for Him. This is what brought an everlasting being with unlimited power to His knees in the Garden. This is what made it hard. This was not a problem God could simply summon more power to overcome. This wasn't a matter of power. This problem, its sacrifice and enduring pain dealt directly with the essence of who God was and is as an eternal being.

Ultimately, there is only one power in the entire universe that could lock horns with God and match His strength. That power is Himself! On the cross God was now at war with Himself. To save His children He needed a part of Himself to take on their sin, but the effect of sin was that it caused separation from God. Do you see it developing now?

Hear Jesus' words again, "Why have you forsaken me?" God is in trouble here. He is literally being ripped apart on this terrible cross, one third of His awesome being screaming

What if God is Like This?

out for the rest of Him, in vain.

This word *forsaken* translates from the Greek word, "EGKATALEIP" which means *to totally abandon* or *desert*. (Strong's #1459) Essentially Jesus is asking His Father, "Where are you?" This takes us back to the Garden of Eden, doesn't it? Wasn't this God's same question to Adam?

Is it possible that God was not just talking to Adam when He asked that question in the garden? After all, clearly God knew where Adam was hiding. Is it possible with those fateful bites of fruit that somewhere God heard the mournful cry of Jesus on the cross? While Adam and Eve could still hear the crunching of the food in their mouths, was God already feeling the effects of that first sin tearing Him apart? Perhaps that is where He first felt the separation of Christ and perhaps it was Jesus He was partially talking to when He asked, "Where are You?"

Can you hear them now? Here are two parts of this divine being, Father and Son, crying out to each other through the centuries, yearning for what had now been displaced.

Combine these two ideas. One that God was literally torn in two on the cross, and the other that there might be a part of God that through Christ is eternally enduring the cross, and suddenly we have God in some sort of eternal position of constant separation from Himself! This is a position of forever having to use His incredible power to hold Himself in a continual state of separated togetherness. How much power does that take? How much power does it take to tear God apart!? And how much more power does it take for Him to still keep Himself together?

But wait, there is still more! Remember as a result of this whole ordeal, Jesus died. Why? Go back to Genesis. What was the punishment of eating from that tree? "…but you must not eat from the tree of the knowledge of good and evil, for when you eat of it you will surely *die*." (Genesis 2:17) Death was one of the consequences of sin. In addition to the already immeasurable price Christ had to pay to save us, He had to die, too.

As if He was not already flexing His muscles enough, how much did the universe warp as God, in a display of might never before witnessed, showed the full extent of His awesome power? Drawing upon unimaginable strength, He became the only creature that was ever powerful enough to bring itself back from the dead! *How much power did that take?*

Is it any wonder Jesus asked for another way? Is it any wonder He sat sweating great drops of blood? What kind of love does it take to pay a price like this? What kind of love does it take to make a sacrifice like this? Only a parent could even begin to understand.

7
What If God Has His Hands Full?

When I really think about the amount of effort Christ put into and perhaps is still putting into the cross, it changes my perspective on why certain things happen, or don't happen in my life. I tend to be a bit more patient with the fact that all of my prayers are not answered the way I would like them to be. I become less critical of God as I learn just how limited my perspective is.

I recall a story from my childhood that helps to illustrate this. Interestingly, it was an incident I never fully understood until I became a parent.

It was one of those rare winter days in southern Arizona

where it actually snowed! And of all days, it was Christmas! Imagine my childhood delight as I awoke that bright morning to find the sunlight glistening off the white winter coat that now blanketed our ranch.

Since snow days were rare, when they came it was not uncommon for my parents to tell us to grab a sled, round everybody up, load the truck, and drive into the nearby mountains to play in the white stuff. That's exactly what happened on one occasion.

On this day we climbed into our old, blue Ford—it was a beast of a truck, an 80's model, full length, King Cab pick-up designed to pull trailers. Along for the ride were my Mom and Dad, my older sister, and my younger sister. We were enjoying the drive up the familiar dirt road and began to ascend the remote mountain that now looked like a foreign landscape under the snow.

About midway up, we reached a stretch of roadway that had become rather treacherous under the winter conditions. The wheels of the truck began to spin out. The vehicle had plenty of torque but was only a two-wheel drive. I remember feeling nervous as I looked out the passenger side window at the steep drop-off that awaited any vehicle that should veer too far to the right.

When it became apparent we were not going to get any further up the road, and that attempting to do so would be extremely dangerous, Dad decided to stop the truck where we were for a moment, to enjoy the view. Mom and Dad got out of the truck along with my older sister, a college student at the time. The truck was still positioned precariously on a steep incline so my parents told me and my little sister to remain in the vehicle with our seatbelts on.

I obeyed, but I remember vividly the anxious feeling I had in the pit of my stomach. As they walked a few steps away to examine the view of the valley far below, I remember being absolutely certain that the truck was going to slide. I don't know what it was about my elementary aged mind that was so sure this was going to occur, but I was certain enough that I told my sister to be ready to take off her seatbelt and jump out if we started to move.

I sat tensely with my finger on the button to release the seatbelt when the world around us began to shift as the massive truck began to slowly slide backwards down the mountain with nothing but a small mound of dirt along the side of the road keeping us from going over the edge. Fortunately the two doors of the truck were still standing open. I yelled at my sister to get out, and the chaos began. I could hear my mother yelling outside the truck as I pushed the front seat forward and jumped out the door. I landed in the soft dirt next to the steep incline and remember feeling squeezed between the truck on one side of my body and the drop off on the other. From my position on the ground I could see under the truck. I saw the legs of my mother and older sister on the other side as they were trying to pull my little sister out of the vehicle. I even remember my older sister slipping and falling backwards on the ground. Her leg was dangerously close to the front left tire that was creeping toward her. She was able to pull back in time to avoid getting run over. I also saw my little sister's tiny legs hit the ground. She was out safely.

With the passenger door still open, I couldn't run to the front of the vehicle as there wasn't enough room to go around the door without falling off the embankment to the right of the truck. This left me with only one direction to run as the heavy door kept moving toward me. I turned and began running down the mountain toward the tail end of the truck, trying to get away from it.

As I made it past the rear bumper, I saw something I will never forget for the rest of my life. It was my father. He was on his knees using all of his strength to shove against the rear bumper of the vehicle. He had slipped in the ice while trying to stop the truck from sliding. Due to this slip, he dropped lower than the tailgate of the truck and therefore, never saw us get out.

Still thinking his two youngest children were in the vehicle, he refused to let go long enough to get to his feet again. He was desperately shoving with all of his might against the

What if God is Like This?

steel bumper as it was pushing him backwards down the mountain. I remember him trying to dig his feet in to the icy road for traction to no avail, frantically trying to save our lives. From this position, he suddenly looked tiny compared to this looming mass of metal that was threatening to either crush him or take him over the edge of the embankment. Fortunately, after a few feet, the vehicle came to a rest.

To this day I don't know if dad was actually successful in stopping the truck or if it stopped on its own. What I do know is that I saw something that I would not fully appreciate until I became a father. I saw the complete reckless abandon of a parent trying to save his children.

My dad has never been the warm, fuzzy type. He was raised as a cowboy on the family ranch. At the age of seventeen he lost his father. He is not what most would consider exceptionally tender, but he is friendly, the type that prefers handshakes to hugs. When it comes to showing love, he's not the most expressive sort, yet in my life nobody has ever told me they loved me louder than he did on that day.

I have to wonder: what if I had been able to run toward the front of the truck, you know, the smart way, the direction opposite the way the truck was sliding? That would have been a much safer direction for me go, but had I done so I would have never seen the effort my father was exerting in order to save our lives. In fact, since he had fallen to his knees, I probably would not have seen him at all.

Imagine *that* scene. I would be standing uphill looking down on the view of the truck sliding away. I would have seen my mother and sister frantically trying to get my little sister out of the truck, but I would have never seen my dad behind the large vehicle. Imagine the perspective I might have had! I might have said, "Look at this! Here my sister and I are in our greatest moment of need and dad takes off! Some father I have, where is he?!" Perhaps I would have felt betrayed or abandon by him. "How dare he leave the entire family in such a time of desperation?" "He even forced his wife and firstborn daughter to risk injury and possibly death to save his kids. Man, what a scum bag!"

How unfortunate that perspective would have been because nothing could have been further from the truth. The very reason I would not have been able to see him would have been due to the extreme levels of effort he was exerting to save me!

I wonder sometimes if this is how it might be with God and our perceptions of Him. Is it possible that one reason we don't see Him the way we want to is due to the immense amount of effort He is exhibiting trying to save us?

How often have we stood by disgusted with Him? Where was He when we needed Him during those difficult times in our lives? Why did the child have to die? Why did my

What if God is Like This?

husband have to leave me? Why wasn't the cancer cured? Why didn't He stop the accident? Why? Why? Why? Why did He leave us when we needed Him most?

Perhaps the answer is just that we are on the wrong side of the truck. We are not able to see His full efforts. Perhaps we don't get to see what we want to see because God is obscured by the very problem itself as He was using every ounce of His unlimited power on our behalf. Perhaps we don't understand because all the while He is groaning under the incredible weight of a terrible and eternal cross, using unimaginable power to hold the very gates of Hell at bay... for us.

8

What If Salvation Is Not Standardized?

"Salvation is found in no one else, for there is no other name under heaven given to men by which we must be saved." (Acts 4:12)

The crickets are chirping on a moonlit night near the Sea of Galilee. The glow of a campfire flickers near the shore and the sounds of night are broken by bursts of laughter and loud voices. Thirteen men sit relaxing around the fire, drinking wine, telling stories and jokes. Suddenly, out of the shadows emerges another figure. It is a man dressed in fine robes. He scans the circle of men which has now grown silent at the presence of their new visitor. He finally locks eyes with the one he has come to see, the one called Jesus. He beckons to Jesus and asks Him if he could speak to Him for a moment in private. Jesus agrees and rises up from the group. As they walk away, the rest of the men begin to murmur, "That's one of the Pharisees! What is he doing here?"

They grow nervous as they fear a possible trap. It was no secret the Pharisees hated Jesus because He was stealing their thunder in front of the masses.

The two men stroll along the shore of the lake as small waves lap against the sand. As they walk, the Pharisee, Nicodemus, nervously begins to search for the words to express his confusion. Unlike the rest of his peers, he senses there is something different about this Jesus guy.

"Rabbi, we know you are a teacher who has come from God. For no one could perform the miraculous signs you are doing if God were not with him."

Jesus grins at Nicodemus for a moment then looks down as He walks. Jesus then turns his face toward his inquisitor and says calmly, "I tell you the truth, no one can see the kingdom of God unless he is born again." (John 3:3)

Nicodemus is surprised. Now more puzzled, he asks, "How can a man be born when he is old? Surely he cannot enter a second time into his mother's womb to be born!" (John 3:4)

Jesus chuckles at this question before stopping along the

shore and looking directly at Nicodemus. With the moonlight dancing in his eyes he responds, "I tell you the truth, no one can enter the kingdom of God unless he is born of water and the Spirit. Flesh gives birth to flesh, but spirit gives birth to spirit. You should not be surprised at my saying, 'You must be born again.'" (John 3:5-7)

The two continue walking for a few moments in silence. A gentle breeze begins to blow in off the waters as Jesus gazes out over the lake and continues. "The wind blows where it pleases. You hear its sound, but you cannot tell where it comes from or where it is going. So it is with everyone born of the Spirit." (John 3:8)

"How can this be?" responds a still baffled Nicodemus. (John 3:9)

"You are Israel's teacher and do you not understand these things?" Jesus ribs gently, "I tell you the truth, we speak of what we know, and we testify to what we have seen, but still you people do not accept our testimony. I have spoken to you of earthly things and you do not believe; how then will you believe if I speak of heavenly things? No one has ever gone into heaven except the one who came from heaven, the Son of Man. Just as Moses lifted up the snake in the desert, so the Son of Man must be lifted up, that everyone who believes in him may have eternal life." (John 3:10-15)

Jesus pauses for a few moments to allow everything he

has just said to sink in as the two conclude their conversation. As they make their way back to the campfire, Nicodemus has much to ponder.

What does one need to do to be *saved*? What is the real answer?

In this story out of John Chapter 3, Jesus tells Nicodemus that he must be "born again" to enter into the kingdom of heaven. We also get the famous John 3:16 that "whoever believes" in God's only Son will "not perish, but have everlasting life."

What is a little unnerving is that if you turn back a few pages in the Bible, to Matthew, Chapter 19, we find Jesus in an encounter with a rather smug and wealthy young politician. When this man asks Jesus, "Teacher, what good thing must I do to get eternal life?" Jesus responds telling him that in order for him to be "perfect," he must sell all his possessions. He must give the proceeds to the poor. Then he will have a "treasure in heaven."

Why didn't Jesus tell this man the same thing he told Nicodemus? Why would he give two people such remarkably different answers about this all-important topic of salvation? What is even more confusing is this: It's a common theme with Jesus to give answers that don't match one another. He seldom, if ever, gives the same response twice when it comes to salvation!

While preparing to send out the twelve disciples in Matthew 10 Jesus says, "All men will hate you because of me, but he who stands firm to the end will be saved." (Matthew 10:22) To the sinful woman in Luke 7 who washes his feet with her hair and tears Jesus says, "Your faith has saved you; go in peace." In Luke 23 the thief on the cross simply asks to be "remembered" to which Jesus replies, "I tell you the truth, today you will be with me in paradise." While addressing a crowd in Acts 2:21 Peter says, "…And everyone who calls on the name of the Lord will be saved."

Houston, we have a problem! Why are there so many diverging answers to this single question of obtaining salvation? In most evangelical churches across America if someone wants to become a Christian they are simply led, typically by a pastor, in a prayer where they confess to God that they are sinners, request forgiveness, and ask Jesus to come into their heart. It is quite a standardized practice actually. However, when we look at Jesus giving multiple and differing answers to many people, it starts to look like there is nothing standard about a method of obtaining salvation.

What if Nicodemus had gone out and told people he heard that they needed to be *born again* and to just *believe* in Jesus to be saved? If people had followed those instructions would they be saved?

What about the rich young ruler? What if he had told the

people in his network that he heard from the very mouth of Jesus himself: "In order to be *perfect* you need to sell all of your possessions and give the proceeds to the poor." If people were to follow those instructions would they be saved?

People watching the thief's interaction with Jesus as both were crucified might have walked away believing they only needed to ask God to be *remembered*, and may have shared that comforting thought with their friends. Others might have become convinced they needed to find a way to wash the feet of Jesus with their hair and tears, difficult at best as Jesus moved around a lot.

The only thing consistent with the answers Jesus gave people, were that the answers were inconsistent. It appears that every response Jesus gave dealt specifically with the issues relating to that particular person only. What if salvation is something that is more personal than simply repeating a prayer? What if it is less about what we do than it is about who we know? After all, Jesus Himself had said, "No one comes to the Father except through me." (John 14:6)

So, what if that is the case? What if salvation is *not* accomplished by repeating some prayer, or doing some task, or believing some creed? What if true salvation is attained *exclusively* by going directly to Jesus and discovering what His tailored answer is for you and you alone?

Maybe that is one reason why Christianity is in such

poor shape in the United States, and in Europe, and in other countries that have heard the Gospel preached and the invitation given. Perhaps thousands of Christians across the globe have just repeated prayers believing that upon the conclusion of that prayer they really are Christians, when in fact they have never experienced a true *relationship* with Christ. What would be the implications of this? Perhaps people like this would say things like, "Lord, when did we see you hungry or thirsty or a stranger, or needing clothes, or sick or in prison, and did not help you?" (Matthew 25:44)

Perhaps these are the ones who believe they are saved when really Jesus has never known them. This would be the equivalent of the man who was a friend of the rich young ruler. What if a man like that went out and sold all he had because that is what the ruler told him Jesus said to do? Perhaps that man's salvation lay on a different path, one in which only Jesus Himself knew.

What if that's the answer?

When Christians deal with salvation we seem to have adopted a prescribed, established, and repetitive method of guiding people toward faith. You can ask just about any Christian person what one must do to be saved and most will say something like, "Ask Jesus to forgive you of your sins." Or, "Ask Jesus to come into your heart." The problem with these very common *Christian* answers is that they are not specifically found in the Bible. Nowhere does it say to "Ask Jesus into your heart." What if Christians are just asking people to repeat what someone else told them?

Let's face it, there are many people out there, perhaps reading this right now, who believe they are *saved* because they were told they would be if they just repeated a prayer. Perhaps they were never directly *sent* to Jesus for their answer. How sickening would that be? To live your entire life only to find you experienced only a shadow of the depth you could have known because you never encountered the actual person who held *the answer for you*?

Wouldn't it make sense that because each of us are different, with our own struggles, our own vices, and our own doubts that each of us may require a slightly different path to salvation, a path that is still grounded on the cross, a path that still must take us through Jesus, but a path unique to us none the less? After all, we each have our own sinful battles to fight.

Each time someone came to Christ, He was able to zero in on their exact heart issue. He was able to immediately isolate what it was that separated them from Him. For the vertically challenged tax collector, Zaccheus, it was his greed, for the adulterous woman it was fidelity, for the rich young ruler it was materialism, for Nicodemus it meant to die to an old legalistic form of religion. Why as people approach Jesus

What if God is Like This?

today would it be any different?

If Christ truly is the answer, then wouldn't He still be able to zero in on our hearts and provide us the direct guidance we need? When you are seeking Christ, what does your heart tell you? What sins and struggles rise to the surface in your life as the result of seeking Him? Often that small voice is the very Christ we think we can't find. It's the voice that whispers things like, "Stop the greed, quit looking at that junk on the internet, get an accountability partner, forgive your neighbor, and let go of the prejudice."

Often it is the very voice we tend to ignore as we try to move on with our lives. What a shame. Christ does speak to us. We just need to listen. When we are honest with ourselves we know exactly what it is we need to work on. If we don't know, then I would question whether or not we have really sought Him. He will push us and guide us to purity—we need only decide whether or not we want to follow or even listen. If we ignore the voice long enough, we will lose the ability to hear it.

We may possess the capacity and the capability to do all kinds of great things, such as feeding the poor, clothing the naked, and tending the sick only to never know the Christ we thought we were serving because we ignored His personal calling on our lives.

Revisit what in my opinion is one of the most terrifying

scriptures in the whole Bible: "Not everyone who says to me, 'Lord, Lord,' will enter the kingdom of heaven, but only he who does the will of my Father who is in heaven. Many will say to me on that day, 'Lord, Lord, did we not prophesy in your name, and in your name drive out demons and perform many miracles?' Then I will tell them plainly, 'I never knew you. Away from me, you evildoers.'" (Matthew 7:21-23)

What an absolutely horrible situation for these people! Here they are, fully expecting to be in God's good graces only to hear Him say He never knew them. Now, as disturbing as this is, the biggest question for me is, "Who are they?" And slightly more important, "How do I know I'm not one of them?"

Obviously they felt they were saved. They were under the impression they were doing the right things. Look at their responses to Christ as they try to validate their faith by pointing out how they drove out demons and even performed miracles! Those facts are pretty amazing, actually. Is it possible that prophesying in Christ's name, driving out demons, and performing miracles are outside of God's will? Notice that the key to this passage is that the only people who will enter into the kingdom of heaven are those who *do the will* of the Father.

So the question now arises: Were these people not doing the will of the Father, or were they not doing the will of the

Father *for their particular lives*? For instance, according to John 10:41, John the Baptist never performed a single miracle, yet Jesus declares in Matthew 11:11, "Among those born of women there has not risen anyone greater than John the Baptist."

Clearly, John the Baptist performed the will of the Father for his life, and clearly, working miracles was not part of the plan *for him*. Is it possible the reason Jesus gave different people unique answers was because God had varied plans for each of their lives?

I believe the fact that each of us exists is a testament that God has a unique plan for all of us. He has a job for each of us to do. We are all gifted with the strengths and tools necessary to complete the plan He has for each one of us.

There are a lot of situations where Christ gives varying tasks to different people. Notice how the disciples were told to follow Jesus, while the man possessed by the legion of demons, recorded in Mark, Chapter 5, was specifically not allowed to go with Jesus, rather, instructed to remain where he was. In order to do the will of the Father in one's life, one would need to know what that will was.

There is only one common denominator in all of these encounters—only one. That one common facet is Jesus, Himself! The answers may have been different, but the person giving those answers was always the same. If somebody wants to connect with God, they have to go straight through Jesus to do so.

Look at what He says in the following verses (italics added): "Jesus answered, 'I am the way and the truth and the life. *No one comes to the Father except through me. If you really knew me, you would know my Father as well...*'" (John 14:6-7) "I am the gate; whoever enters *through me* will be saved..." (John 10:9)

I've heard it said, "Jesus is the answer" but I think a more appropriate phrase could be, "Jesus *has* the answer!" Only He knows the complete will of the Father. In order to learn that will for my life I must go directly to Him. In order to learn that will for your life you must go directly to Him. The relationship with Christ must be a direct one for me and a direct one for you.

Let's learn from the misfortunes of seven rather unfortunate and bumbling brothers in the Book of Acts, Chapter 19. The context: God did extraordinary miracles through the Apostle Paul, so that even handkerchiefs and aprons that had touched him were taken to the sick, and their illnesses were cured and the evil spirits left them. Some Jews who practiced driving out evil spirits tried to invoke the name of the Lord Jesus over those who were demon possessed. They would say, "In the name of Jesus, whom Paul preaches, I command you to come out." Seven sons of Sceva, a Jewish chief priest, were doing this. One day the evil spirit answered them, "Jesus I know, and I know about Paul, but who are you?" Then the man who had the evil spirit jumped on them and overpowered them all. He gave them such a beating that they ran out of the house naked and bleeding. (Acts 19:11-16) Can you believe these guys?! Here they are, jealous of all this attention Paul is getting and they decide to get their piece of the pie. They try to take the short cut and begin to cast out demons via third person and it almost gets them killed.

How many of us do the same thing, though? How many of us plan to get to heaven by believing in the Jesus my parents believe in, or my pastor believes in, or my friend believes in?

We have to be careful if we tell people that they *only* have to *believe* in Jesus in order to be *saved*. It is pretty clear: Those poor people may someday stand before Christ at the judgment thinking they are redeemed because they believed in him. James addresses this misconception in his writings when he writes, "Even the demons believe, and they shudder."

It's more than just believing! It's doing! Just like believing you are married doesn't make a marriage. I'm afraid we practice faith in an American church culture where a number of people are present who believe in Jesus, but that's about it. Do we really know if our relationship with Jesus is legitimate? Are we just going through some motions, or are we really truly, actively, seeking out the living breathing God? The fact is, whoever Jesus is talking about when He speaks of those who will begin to ramble off their resume of good works at the golden gates are real people! This is really going to happen to someone!

Look at this verse: "Enter through the narrow gate. For wide is the gate and broad is the road that leads to destruction, and many enter through it. But small is the gate and narrow the road that leads to life, and only a few find it." (Matthew 7:13-14) Upon close examination we start to see that perhaps there is a discrepancy between the number of people who call themselves followers of Christ and the number who really are.

One of the greatest criticisms about Christians is that they are "hypocrites." We hear this name calling all the time. But let's be realistic: one of the reasons this is said about us is because many of us are. There is a marked difference between the guy who is trying to seek God and just messes up, and to the person who proclaims they are Christian but does nothing to invest into that relationship with God.

Who are you following today? Can you, as a Christian, really say that you have sought out Christ and are allowing His Spirit to guide you as to the will of the Father in your life? Or is it possible that you are like the seven of sons of Sceva and are trying to follow God's plan for someone else?

If we never actually seek out our own personal relationship with Jesus, then we are simply following the faith of those who might have influence in our lives. If you are not personally following Christ and His teachings, then you may be simply following a religion. Jesus is not a religion! He is a living, loving being who has paid an enormous price for us, who has given each of us the free will to choose whether or not we want to respond, love Him back, and enter into His kingdom.

9
The Big Decision

"Life is a sum of all your choices." ~Albert Camus

Life is filled with decisions and choices. Some might be as easy as, "Yes, I think I will take another breath." Others might be more difficult, such as whether or not to hit the snooze button again. In essence, everything we do is just one decision and choice after another. Am I going to be lazy or will I work hard? Am I going to be a pessimist or an optimist? Will I be kind or cold hearted? Will I seek first to love, or to be loved? On and on we could go.

When I look at my life, I see factors over which I had no control. Among them: who my parents and siblings would be, where I would grow up, my race, my height, my early education, my neighbors, and so on. From my earliest memory I can recount about five to ten decisions that were so significant that they were pivotal in the direction of my life. I think most of us can look at our lives and say the same thing. We can look back and trace most of our struggles and most of our successes to a couple of fateful moments: that decision to drop out of school, to stay in school, to join the military, to go to college, to have sex, to get married, to break up, to get drunk that one night, to try drugs, to resist peer pressure and succeed, to take that job, to move to a different town, to buy that house, or to try that investment. Which ones were they for you?

Some of life's choices cause people to place a significant amount of thought into what they are choosing. There are times where being impulsive can be a dangerous thing, and other times when impulsiveness doesn't amount to much. Typically, the bigger the decision the more thought you want to put into it.

For some reason this doesn't seem to be a philosophy that many churches buy into. Or, at least they don't seem by buy into it when it comes to the biggest possible decision a person could ever make: deciding who my God will be.

When we examine the Great Commission of Christ documented at the conclusion of the Book of Matthew, we see that the calling was to "…go and make disciples of all nations…" Somehow over the years Christians have reconfigured this verse into this: "Go and make 'converts' of all nations." While we read in the Bible of people dramatically dropping to their knees and making radical decisions to follow Christ after encounters with Christians, I'm not sure this is a practical objective for us to strive for today.

Now before you put this book down or throw it in a fire for being blasphemous, hear me out. I am one who believes people should avoid rushing into big decisions whenever possible. This is something that I hope most of us can agree upon. But why is it that when it comes to the biggest decision and choice a person can make, to follow Christ or not, we feel the need to close the deal quickly and push them into a commitment? We want people to sit down at a church service, and within an hour make a decision to "Give their life to Christ." That's great and all, but let's back up a second and examine this more thoroughly.

Suppose I have a single friend named Larry whom I know very well. And let's say I get on a bus and I meet a single young lady named Sally. Over the course of the ride, I get to visiting with Sally and quickly determine that Larry would be a great husband for her. How absolutely preposterous would it be for me to suggest to Sally that she marry my friend, Larry? What would be even crazier? If she decided to say, "Yes! In fact, let's call him right now and set the wedding date!"

Anybody who heard this story would tell you that this

marriage probably would stand little chance of success. Yet, this is exactly what we ask people to do all the time when it comes to a relationship with Christ. If they don't choose right then and in the way we want them to, we shake our heads in disgust. We become annoyed, maybe discouraged when we see the number of people out there who give up on Christ or have a weak and shallow faith, yet many times, we are the very ones who have set them up to fail! It truly is, "Easy come, easy go."

The decision to accept Christ and to choose to follow the teachings of Christ *shouldn't be easy*! In reality, shouldn't a person at the very least put the same amount of thought and consideration into a relationship with Christ as they would into a marriage, or the purchase of a home, or anything else of great and lasting consequence? Someone might say, "Well, what about those split-second conversions that took place in the Bible? Weren't those valid?"

That is a very good question. What about the jailer of Paul and Silas, or the Ethiopian eunuch, and others in the New Testament that made immediate decisions for Christ? There is one very significant difference between the split-second conversions in many parts of the world today and the split-second conversions of the early church era. It is this: In the early church era a person knew that they were risking their very life with the decision they were about to make. It was no secret to anybody that the followers of Christ were, at the very least, going to be persecuted and, at worst, could be stoned to death, crucified, tortured, imprisoned, and in some instances even turned into lion bait in the Roman Coliseum. These people understood quickly the fullness and ramifications of the decisions they were making. They had become already aware of the fact that the choice to follow Christ could be nothing short of a death sentence. A choice to convert may have meant that they had signed their own death warrant.

Let's face it: that kind of thing doesn't exist anymore in many places in the world, especially in the Western Hemisphere, and let's be thankful that it doesn't. Just because spit-second decisions were recorded in scripture doesn't mean these were not big decisions and deliberate choices. People knew what was being asked of them; they knew even more what the consequences of their choices could be. Today, we have the obligation to both people and to God, to make sure potential converts are aware of the magnitude of the decision they are about to make. People need to know Jesus is asking an entire life of devotion from them. People need to be fully aware of the magnitude of what it is they are doing. Didn't Jesus Himself preach of first considering the cost?

Luke 14:26-33: "If anyone comes to me and does not hate his father and mother, his wife and children, his brothers and sisters—yes, even his own life—he cannot be my disciple. And anyone who does not carry his cross and follow me cannot be my disciple."

"Suppose one of you wants to build a tower. Will he not first sit down and estimate the cost to see if he has enough money to complete it? For if he lays the foundation and is not able to finish it, everyone who sees it will ridicule him, saying, 'This fellow began to build and was not able to finish.'"

"Or suppose a king is about to go to war against another king. Will he not first sit down and consider whether he is able with ten thousand men to oppose the one coming against him with twenty thousand? If he is not able, he will send a delegation while the other is still a long way off and will ask for terms of peace. In the same way, any of you who does not give up everything he has cannot be my disciple."

Or how about this one?

Mark 8:34-35, "Then he called the crowd to him along with his disciples and said: 'If anyone would come after me, he must deny himself and take up his cross and follow me. For whoever wants to save his life will lose it, but whoever loses his life for me and for the gospel will save it.'"

It's interesting that when people are coming down to the alters at the front of churches to the tune of "Just As I Am" these are not typically the first scripture passages that are shared with them. None of this is to say that we shouldn't encourage people to choose to follow Christ when we present our faith to them, but the last thing we should do is try to rile people up into immense emotional frenzies and then pressure them to make what will be by far the most important and life-altering decision of their entire existence.

Essentially, when we push it or rush it we turn the salvation decision into a Las Vegas wedding in which people make a huge choice while intoxicated by emotion only to wake up the next morning and wonder what they have gotten themselves into. Such actions under the banner of winning people to Christ have led to a number of weak and shallow churches, and actions like these run the risk of attempting to take the work of salvation into our own hands because we have either counted the cost and don't care, or we have not counted the cost at all because of fear.

We need to be comfortable enough to present people the Gospel as it stands, and be transparent enough to let them see our own struggles as we "work out" our salvation "with fear and trembling." (Philippians 2:12) We need to be able to direct people to Christ, and allow His Spirit to work in such a way as to bring to the surface the issues in their lives.

In our churches when we lead people in our standard "Sinner's Prayer" while we are leading them onto the right path, we also must try to assure that these converts understand they are at the beginning of the road, not its end, that this is the wedding, not the marriage.

10
What If God Has a Treasure?

> "Do not store up for yourselves treasures on earth, where
> moth and rust destroy, and where thieves break in and steal.
> But store up for yourselves treasures in heaven,
> where moth and rust do not destroy, and where thieves
> do not break in and steal. For where your treasure is,
> there your heart will be."
> (Matthew 6:19-21)

If you have grown up in church, how many times have you heard these words? One of the reasons this passage is so powerful is simply because it's true. If you want to know what really is important to you, take a look at where your heart is. What do you long for, what do you spend your time doing, or, even better, what do you spend your time wishing you were doing? What do you drop everything for? When your life is over, to what causes and activities will you have committed the greatest amount of your energy, resources, and effort? Answer those questions, and you will know what your treasure is.

What a brilliant tool Jesus gave us, to analyze our lives. The tool was also a great warning, too, spelling out the dangers of treasuring things of little value. The warning is: Be careful what you choose as your treasure because your heart will follow. Invest your life in things that matter.

This tool can also act as a measuring stick others can use on us. We can claim something is important to us, but ultimately people will be able to see where our heart really rests. It is hard to hide what we truly treasure because it is revealed in the things we say and do. This is a two-edged sword: it either validates what we claim about ourselves, or proves us to be hypocrites.

What an incredibly self-reflective nugget of wisdom Jesus has shared with us. What I love about this passage is that it's true for everybody. Even Jesus, Himself, was subject to this statement. Jesus knew better than anybody that a heart will dwell with its treasures because Jesus had His treasures, too.

Did you know that? Well you should, because Jesus' treasure is *you*. You are His treasure because you are where

His heart dwells! You don't need to earn God's approval or His attention, you already hold His heart.

I wonder what it was like when Jesus actually spoke these words. Did He pause momentarily? Did He choke up? Perhaps His eyes got watery? Think about the significance of His sharing these words to the crowd—He was essentially expressing His love to them. "Store up your treasures in Heaven," He begins, "for where your treasure is, there your heart will be." Strange isn't it? He was revealing so much about Himself in this sentence. Isn't that the exact reason He came? Isn't that why he paid that horrendous penalty on the cross? He did all of it to store up His treasure in Heaven, to make a way for all of us to go to there and dwell with Him.

Yes, Jesus knew what He was talking about. He was giving us a little window into His own heart. He was once again telling us how much He loves us. We are nothing short of a valuable treasure in His eyes! You and I mean the world to Him; check that, you and I *are* the world to Him!

Now the question remains, what is He to you? It is no wonder Paul writes: "For I am convinced that neither death nor life, neither angels nor demons, neither the present nor the future, nor any powers, neither height nor depth, nor anything else in all creation, will be able to separate us from the love of God that is in Christ Jesus our Lord." (Romans 8:38-39)

He is right. God is so strong that Satan can't stop Him by deceiving mankind, sin can't stop Him, and not even death itself can thwart His love. In fact the only thing in the world that can possibly separate us from His incredible love is our own free will. Just as it was in the Garden of Eden, it comes back to our choice: whether we want to love Him back, or not. The price on the cross has been paid. He has atoned for our sins but the battle isn't over.

We are now in a very similar position to that of Adam and Eve in the Garden of Eden. We have a choice to make, and again He has granted us the freedom to choose as we please. Remember why He made that Tree of the Knowledge of Good and Evil? It was to give us a choice, and with that choice, the ability to love Him as well as the ability to sin. The fact is, Jesus loves us so much that on our behalf He subjected himself to suffering we will never understand. But he also loves us so much He won't take away our choice, our freedom, our ability to love, and our ability to sin. This is love, this is freedom.

If we decide we don't want to love Him or be with Him, we are free to make that choice. But I think it is pretty clear: God loves us deeply — all He really wants in return is what any other parent would want. He just wants His kids to love Him back.

Look at Jesus' response when asked about the greatest commandment. "Love the Lord your God with all your heart and with all your soul and with all your mind, and with all your strength." (Mark 12:30) Why would he ask us to love Him with all of our heart, soul, mind, and strength? Because that's exactly the same way He loves us.

11
True Love

Every time I walk though the checkout line at the grocery store I'm visually assaulted by the latest Hollywood gossip. An assortment of magazines offer to educate me how to improve my love life, tell me the top twenty things women want, reveal which famous people are getting married or divorced, and which famous people are cheating on their famous significant others. With all these magazine tips you would think that every marriage in America should be blossoming!

It's ironic how often I see the word *love* thrown around so loosely in their headlines. I often feel like the love life of Hollywood is on par with that of some students in a typical high school. Thankfully, all I have to do is make it through the checkout line and the shallowness ends. After all, it's not like I have to drive home past a bunch of foolish billboards using sex to sell any product you can think of. And when I get home, thankfully I can turn on the old TV for a little rest and relaxation and not have to worry about commercials claiming that the love of my life is waiting for me on a website, or about how wonderful certain enhancement products might work, or that the Thursday night lineup will contain hormone-charged reality shows geared toward teenagers, shows about groups of people fighting over each other in order to win a rose of affection (and those are the tame ones).

As a parent, society terrifies me with the messages it blitzes toward my kids about this thing called *love*. My grandparents were married for 69 years before my grandfather passed away. My parents are approaching their 50th, and I have several aunts and uncles who are now past 50 years in their marriages. I don't understand why these aren't the types of people those magazines interview or reality shows follow. Instead the media turns to the most dysfunctional people in society to act as beacons of guidance about the most important relationships in our lives. I'm afraid that as a society we have lost our compass when it comes to love.

It really makes you wonder: Would we recognize true love if we saw it? After all, what is true love? Really? How often have you thought about it? Have you ever truly experienced it? For most of my life I thought I had but things have changed. I recently came to the realization that my perspective on love had been deeply skewed.

When I think back over my relatively limited number of years on this earth, I have come to the realization that the people I have come closest to loving have been my children. Every other relationship in my life that I thought was based on love really never was. Love as I knew it has been nothing more than an illusion. I hate to admit it, but I now realize I never really loved my parents, I never really loved my family, I really didn't love any of the people I called friends growing up. I didn't love my wife when I met her, I didn't love her when I proposed to her, I didn't love her when I stood at an altar and told her I loved her. But I thought I did. In fact, throughout our marriage I thought I loved her deeply, but I have since learned that I was wrong about what I thought love was. In fact, I was robbing her of the true depth of love she deserved due to my limited mindset.

This new perspective came as the result of a day I spent with a good friend of mine just walking around a mall, visiting and talking with each other. Through our conversations I suddenly felt as if a veil had been lifted from my eyes and I realized how amazingly selfish I had been my entire life.

My friend and I were discussing the complexities and

frustrations of marriage. I had just been in a fight with my wife (she was wrong) and he had recently been through a very difficult divorce. (Ok, maybe I was wrong…I don't remember.) Anyway, as we were talking, the topic of God came up and I shared with him that I believed the family unit was the greatest analogy man can use to attempt to understand God's love for us.

The first part of the analogy is the parent-child relationship. As a parent, I realize my children have freewill. I can attempt to raise them to live what I believe is a good life, but as they get older their freewill will win out and they will live according to their choosing.

The thing that is special about my kids, though, is that I can say with full confidence that no matter what or how they choose to live their lives, I will always love them. My love for them is not based on anything other than the fact that they are my children. Nothing they do can add or take away from that. I just love them because they are mine. If my children were to grow up and decided they hated me, if they were to get married and have children of their own and choose another set of parents to go home to, and deny ever knowing me, I would be deeply wounded. I would be hurt, but I would still love them. Why? Because my love for them is based on who they are, not what they do or how they make me feel. I believe this is the love that God feels for us.

What if God is Like This?

The second part of the family analogy is found in the husband-wife relationship. Throughout the Bible, marriage is used to describe God's relationship with mankind, specifically the relationship God had with Israel in the Old Testament and the Church in the New Testament.

The Old Testament contains a book about a Prophet named Hosea. In the Book of Hosea the prophet is directed by God to take an adulterous woman as his wife. This woman named Gomer bears the prophet three children. Many Bible scholars suggest that these children were conceived outside of the marriage due to her reputation for being unfaithful. Finally, the prophet actually has to purchase back her freedom, to bring her home after she had left him.

This marriage is meant to symbolize the type of marriage God had with Israel and I believe to some extent, all of mankind. Time and time again we forsake Him, cheat on Him by giving our hearts to other things, and express our worship to the "other gods" of money and selfishness. God puts up with our unfaithfulness, and even though we ignore Him most of the time, He is still willing to purchase back His bride's freedom at the cross of Christ.

My friend and I began discussing the insanity of Hosea actually marrying an adulterous woman. What kind of a guy would ever do this? How could anybody ever really love someone who was constantly unfaithful to them?

That's when suddenly everything made sense. Hosea did not marry Gomer because he was *in love* with her. Instead, he married her with the *intention* of loving her! The difference is so profound. By marrying her with the intention of loving her, it didn't really matter what she did in the relationship. In fact, it would appear that Hosea fully expected that Gomer would not be faithful to him. But for Hosea, her unfaithfulness didn't matter. It didn't matter because he was not marrying her for anything she provided him. He essentially had decided to take someone who had never experienced true love, and give that kind of love to her.

When this truth hit me, I became profoundly aware of just how selfish I had always been in my marriage and how that selfishness had been the source of every marital frustration I have ever had. You see, when I met my wife and *fell in love* with her I was not falling in love at all. In fact the very opposite was true. When I was around her I felt this wonderful euphoria of emotion that I mistook as love. Honestly, I was attracted to the euphoria I experienced when I was with her, not the genuine appreciation for her whether we were together or not.

Think about it: Why do we love some people and not others? Why do we choose some to be spouses or friends but not others? The reason we choose these people is because of how they make us feel. So really, it's still about us! Every friendship I have ever had was ultimately rooted in selfishness because I accepted or rejected people based on how they made me feel. It was conditional.

Think about traditional wedding vows. We stand up there and tell another person in front of God and everybody that we will stand by them no matter what until the day of our death. But really, we normally don't mean that. What we really mean is, "I will remain all these things to you until I die, as long as you are for me, as well." We don't go into marriages with the idea that even if my spouse cheats on me with a hundred other people that I will still stand by them.

Truly unconditional love is just that, love without conditions. And if there are no conditions, then ultimately, there is nobody we could not love in this manner. Love becomes a proactive choice to bestow on others rather than a reactive emotion based on what others provide us.

Now let me clarify that I'm not promoting that people remain in horribly dysfunctional relationships where they are constantly betrayed and mistreated; rather, I am using an extreme example to convey this concept. In fact, if one were in an above described relationship a strong case could be made that out of love they could or should dissolve the relationship so they would not act as an enabler for the dysfunctional behavior of the spouse. Where horribly dysfunctional relationships are not the issue, the question then becomes, "What is the motivation for the relationship?" Is it genuine love or just the shallow attraction that follows initial impressions?

I began thinking of all the things that have caused problems in my marriage and realized they were all a result of my inability to love my wife unconditionally. If she made me angry I would withhold my love. In actuality, I wanted her to evoke the emotion she did when we first started dating. I became aware that I determined it was up to her to make me continually feel the effects of the euphoric drug of being the center of her world. Even times when I would selflessly give love when I didn't feel like it were only with the hope that she would do the same for me. It was selfishness in the deepest sense.

If real love is truly unconditional, then one should be able to apply it to anybody on earth. To say that I can love one person unconditionally but not another by its very nature proves that conditions are present. Unconditional love really doesn't exist unless it is applied to all people. To say otherwise would mean that some condition exists that prevents me from loving someone. If there is a condition that allows me to love one and not another, then even the love I have for the one is not really unconditional.

What if someone was to master this type of real and pure love, this true and unconditional love? What would that person look like? Well, that person would have made the decision that their entire goal was to love other people and truly and honestly not seek or expect anything in return. That person would be completely and totally selfless. He or she would be completely impervious to pressure from peers because peer pressure derives its power from its desire to be accepted by others. But if this person loved others with absolutely no expectation of getting anything in return, then the acceptance of others would not be an issue. By loving others unconditionally, acceptance by others would no longer be a condition to love; therefore, one would be free from the pressure to be accepted. One could do what was right in their heart, knowing that they will still love their friends even if their friends withheld their acceptance.

This person could be completely honest with others, telling them the truth in love no matter how much that truth might distance the loved one from them. The primary goal would be for the loved one to hear the truth, rather than to make sure the loved one would still like or accept them. Again, being liked or accepted in return would not matter; it would not even be a consideration because the primary focus would be to love not expecting or wanting anything in return.

This person's love would not be affected by acceptance or rejection, by honesty or dishonesty, by loyalty or betrayal. Forgiveness would abound from someone like this because nothing would exist to hold it back. Their selfless love for others would lead this person to always do the right thing. This would be a person who had the ability to perceive how every action would affect others, negatively and positively, and as a result they would always choose to act in the best interests of those around them.

Essentially this person would master every part of their life by simply perfecting one thing: the ability to love unconditionally. Hmm, this sounds a lot like a guy that lived 2,000 years ago.

12
A Return to Freedom

I think if we were honest we would all have to admit we have experienced the prisons that sin constructs. For some of us, sin actually may have landed us in a physical prison, while for others it was walled enclosure of guilt or shame. Perhaps our past decisions and choices continue to haunt us through current situations or with lingering regrets.

In John, Chapter 8, Jesus encountered a woman that we can probably all relate to, at least to some degree. She was caught in the prison of her sin and it was about to pay for it with her life. In a cloud of dust and with shouting voices the Pharisees made their entrance. A woman, barely clothed, with mangled hair and dirt smudged on her face, had been brought to Christ and thrown at His feet. We don't know much about her, only that she was caught in the middle of what was probably the greatest mistake she'd ever made.

Are we really much different than her? Perhaps we weren't caught in adultery, but what if we were caught right in the middle of acts in life for which we are most ashamed? What if everybody knew our darkest secrets? Interestingly, the man she was caught having the affair with is nowhere to be found in the account. Conveniently, only the woman is brought to Christ. This fact has led some to speculate that she was a pawn in a plan to trap Jesus. In the account the religious leaders point out to Jesus that Moses required this woman to be stoned to death for her indiscretion. Should Jesus condone the killing of this woman He will become a wanted man by the Romans for initiating an execution. If He should free her, He will lose all credibility with His followers by going against the Law of the Exodus Prophet. It appears the Pharisees have Him right where they want Him. They have placed Jesus in the perfect catch-22: either answer takes care of their problem. One answer gets Jesus executed, the other answer causes everyone to fall away from him, robbing him of his audience and His influence, ridding the Pharisees of their competition.

Jesus stands for a moment locking eyes with the Pharisees before looking down at this woman cowering before him.

What if God is Like This?

Jesus then stoops to the ground and begins writing in the sand with his finger. The woman's sobs are the only sound now as the crowd grows silent, straining to see what Jesus is writing. After a few moments Jesus stands up and returns his eyes to the religious leaders, most of which are still staring down at whatever he wrote. He then stuns them as he grants permission to anyone without sin to throw the first stone.

With His one statement, Jesus clears the scene, leaving only Him, the woman, and a pile of rocks. He is alone with her. Now He has His chance. Now He can really give her a piece of His mind and let her know what a terrible person she is. Now He can tell her that she deserves to be struck down by God and will someday burn in the fires of Hell!

Time seems to stop for this young lady as she waits for an answer or a comment from Christ. After what seems like an eternity, Jesus stands up from doodling in the sand some more. In my mind's eye, I imagine the woman is unable to lift her head. She is staring to the ground, her eyes containing shame and regret as they swell with tears. I imagine Jesus staring at her for a few moments, first with a slight smile that warms to a wide and encouraging grin. After realizing that she was not going to look at him, I imagine him placing his hand under her chin, lifting her head a little as he stoops to make eye contact with her. "Woman, where are they?" he asks, "Has no one condemned you?"

With a quivering lip she replies in a cracked voice, "No one, sir."

"Then, neither do I condemn you. Go now, and leave your life of sin."

That is Jesus! *That* is the Christ! He is a breaker of chains, a forgiver of sins, and a restorer of dignity! John 3:17 states that Jesus came to *save* the world, He did not come to *condemn* it. Nowhere does He prove this verse more true and relevant than in this story. We all have experienced the freedom *to* sin, but we have not all experienced the freedom *from* sin, and that is what He came to bring us.

Fast forward a few verses in this same chapter and we find Jesus in another verbal battle with the Pharisees, only this time it is Jesus who is on offense. Jesus gets their attention, beginning this scenario by claiming to be the "light of the world." The Pharisees are trying to challenge Jesus on His credibility and credentials to make such claims. At one point in the conversation Jesus turns to His followers and has this exchange:

To the Jews who had believed him, Jesus said, "If you hold to my teaching, you are really my disciples. Then you will know the truth, and the truth will set you free." They (the Pharisees) answered him, "We are Abraham's descendants and have never been slaves of anyone. How can you say that we shall be set free?" Jesus replied, "I tell you the truth, everyone who sins is a slave to sin. Now a slave has no permanent place in the family, but a son belongs to it forever. So if the Son sets you free, you will be free indeed…" (John 8:31-36)

The reply of the Pharisees in which they claim they have never been slaves is nearsighted; the Jews were under Roman occupation at this very time! Their response also seems to ignore one of the most defining situations in Jewish history: their Egyptian captivity which set up the Exodus of Moses, followed by their Assyrian, Babylonian, Persian, and Syrian persecutors as well. But who's to be bothered by minor historical details like that?

In this passage, Jesus articulates his desire for man to be free. The Book of John is a fascinating book for a number of reasons, but one of those reasons is found in the significance of two particular words. The words *light* and *truth* carry great meaning all through this book. As mentioned, Jesus calls himself the "light of the world" in John 8:12. Interestingly, wherever the word *light* is found in John it is almost always a direct reference to Christ.

In John 14:6, Jesus gives us this statement, "I am the way and the truth, and the life. No one comes to the Father except through me." Here Jesus refers to Himself as "the truth." So, guess what happens when you find the word *truth* in the Book of John? It is also a direct reference to Christ. Essentially in this passage Jesus was saying, "If you hold to my teachings, you are really my disciples. Then you will know the truth (*Me*) and the truth (*I*) will set you free." The consistency of the thought continues as Jesus goes on to say, "So if the *Son* sets you free, you will be free indeed."

On June 11, 1966, Frank Lee Morris along with brothers, John and Clarence Anglin, performed one of the most daring and famous escapes of all time. All three were serving sentences on the dreaded island penitentiary of Alcatraz. Through an elaborate plan that took months to devise, they slipped through a hole they had created in the back of their cells, climbed to the roof of the prison, and used a homemade raft made of rain coats to attempt to make it to shore. Nobody ever heard from the men after their escape, leading many to believe they didn't survive the harsh waters of San Francisco Bay. But if they did survive, one thing is clear: once they attained freedom, they never went back! How foolish would it have been if they had made it to shore only to turn themselves back in again! Yet, many of us do exactly that after Christ frees us from our sins. He breaks our sin chains only for us to forge them again and put them right back on.

Is it any wonder that the Apostle Peter wrote that a man who returns to sin is like a dog that returns to its vomit or a washed pig that returns to the mud? (2 Peter 2:22) Why would anyone ever want to put the chains of slavery back on again after having been released?

Jesus came not to hold us all accountable for our sins but rather to free us from the bondage of sin. We are already being held accountable for our sins. The natural result of sinning holds us accountable. We are already condemned. We are held captive to the outcomes of our actions. We don't need someone to hold us accountable; we need someone to free us from the accountability that we are now experiencing as a result of sin.

That is why Jesus came! He came to free us from the captivity of sin and return us to the state in which God had prepared and always had intended for us. Jesus sets us free from legalistic church law, the chains of sin, guilt, and shame, bitterness and hate, and the fear of death! He came to give us life that we might have it to the full! (John 10:10)

There is a better way to live and He has come to show it to us. It is selfless, caring, and forgiving. It is noble, humble, and loving. And it is simply found in love.

Live the life that Jesus taught, love the way He loved, and you will return to freedom! As the author of Galatians exclaimed, "It is for *freedom* that Christ has set us *free*. Stand firm, then, and do not let yourselves be burdened again by a yoke of slavery." (Galatians 5:1)

What if that is what God is like? What if He is more about love than condemnation? What if He is more about freedom than rules? Instead of the Judge issuing a sentence, what if He is more like the Father who desperately pursues His children? What if God is like this?

Conclusion

There's an old story about a politician who was scheduled to give an important speech. He had done something to upset one of his speech writers to the point that the speech writer had decided to quit. The speech writer knew that the politician had to give a very technical talk on a subject the politician knew very little about. So for his final act before resigning, the speech writer prepared the talk for the politician.

The politician arrived at his speaking engagement and was handed the speech just as he was walking onto the stage in front of hundreds of people. The politician began reading his notes and stated in the introduction of the speech that he was going to address several very specific points in the talk. When he turned the next page all that was written was, "You're on your own now!" The remaining pages were blank!

I think many of us can relate to feeling that way about God. He gives us enough information to make a strong case that He exists, but then after that leaves us on our own to try to figure out the most important aspects of life as well as the questions we continue to ask.

For thousands of years people have been trying to figure out who God is and what He is really like. One needs only to look around at the world and all the different religions and belief systems to see the evidence of this.

There are a lot of things about God I believe we will never know in this life, but I am also convinced that He has revealed a lot more about Himself than we give Him credit for. We just need to learn to better see His tracks in our sand.

When I think deeply about freedom, it makes more sense than ever why God functions the way He does. In fact, for me it even explains why He is invisible. Would we really live the same way if we could look up in the sky and see God peering down over our shoulders? He doesn't do that; He doesn't coerce obedience. He creates an environment of liberation so that every choice we make can be genuine and true, so that love can abound in a relationship of uninhibited freedom.

When sin worked its way into the scenario and stole our freedom, God in His infinite love and power stepped in like a father, protecting his child by paying an incomprehensible price to preserve the child's opportunity to enjoy that freedom. He also set the example of what that freedom could look like for us, through the example of the life of Christ.

In the end I believe that our quest for God is not in realms unknown; rather, it is plainly out front so we can see Him clearly. We already have what we are looking for, all around us.

As supernatural creatures living in a supernatural world we have been given a supernatural message and the supreme example of love. As messed up as things sometimes seem, I can't help but wonder if maybe God created the perfect environment for us to experience our freedom to its fullest in fulfillment of His perfect plan.

Acknowledgements

I thank my wife, Karra, for her patience with me during the process of writing this book. I know I was not always easy to deal with, appearing occasionally from behind a computer for several months during the writing and publishing phases. I also thank my kids for sharing their daddy with the keyboard.

To my mom and dad: thanks for a great upbringing established in hard work, that helps "preserve our freedom."

Pastor Brian: thank you for your mentoring, support, and for giving me a place on your staff.

Father Mike: thanks for challenging me to look at things from different perspectives and to think outside my box.

Norm: thanks for introducing me to the Gila…I can't pay

you back for that one.

Jim Ireland: thanks for all the encouragement and the Sunday morning talks where we'd bounce different ideas around.

Gary: thanks a ton for all your help on the website and with my computer illiteracy.

I also want thank all the great people at Creative Team Publishing: Glen Aubrey, Jordan Tementozzi, Jeff Goble, Ashlee Mayo, and Justin Aubrey. You helped make the publication of my first book an easy process, and I'm grateful to you.

The Author

Will Hathaway is a man who has worn many hats. Born the third of four children to a hardworking cattle rancher and his wife near the foothills of the Patagonia Mountains in southern Arizona, he quickly learned what it meant to work with the tools God gave you, your hands. He spent most of his childhood and young adult years driving fence posts and breaking horses.

It wasn't until Will left home to attend Grand Canyon University in Phoenix that he realized how unique his upbringing truly had been. While pursuing a Marketing/Business degree he met and then married the love of his life, Karra. It was through Karra that he obtained his first job in ministry, cleaning toilets at his church and serving as Youth

Pastor to Junior and Senior High School students.

In 1999, Will felt led to pursue his lifelong passion of full-time ministry and headed off to attend Grace Theological Seminary in Warsaw, Indiana. Although he enjoyed his schooling, he took advantage of an offer to take a full-time position as a family life minister for a large church in Blytheville, Arkansas. Will and Karra remained in Arkansas for a year when they were surprised by the news of the upcoming birth of their first child.

They moved back to Arizona to be near family for the new baby. Will took a job in the investing/insurance market, but this vocation left him feeling empty and unfulfilled. During this time he continued his ministry pursuits as a volunteer youth pastor for their local church. The horrible events of 9/11/2001 became deciding factors that ended his short career as an investor.

Soon after, news started to spread that several local fire and police departments were hiring so, on a whim, he took a chance and was hired on as a police officer at a local department. Since his introduction to the police department in 2002, Will has served in many capacities including as a SWAT negotiator.

Through the changes in his life, two things have remained consistent: 1) his call to ministry, with more than fourteen years in ministry beginning as a junior high and high school youth pastor and eventually as a college and career pastor; 2) his passion for his career in law enforcement.

Will is a family man with a strong sense of loyalty, especially when it comes to his wife, Karra, and their three children. He is an avid outdoorsman who enjoys spending time backpacking and camping in the New Mexico Wilderness. Many times he can be seen breaking horses on his parent's ranch, which still runs cattle today.

Will's diverse and multifaceted backgrounds provide him with unique perspectives on the world and God's interaction with it. Always seeking to gain a better understanding of his Creator, he is willing to ask the tough questions, one of which is, "What If God Is Like This?"

Speaking Engagements and Products

Schedule Will Hathaway to speak at your event. Will Hathaway speaks for church services, conferences, Christian camps, and retreats.

Contact Will Hathaway at
www.Will-Hathaway.com

Products:

- *What If God Is Like This?* is the first book in Will's series entitled, *Released From Religion*.

- ***The Human Side of Christ: The Guy behind the God*** is the second book of the series. This book peels back the divine cloak of mystery surrounding Christ and His existence as God in the flesh, and focuses on the human personality that walked the earth. It asks, "Who was this man?" "What was He like?" "How can we relate to Him?" Momentarily view Christ as a man rather than as God and relate to Him human-to-human in very special and basic ways. Discover that studying His humanity actually enhances the perspective of His divinity.

- ***When Dead Men Walk: The Return to Authentic Humanity*** is the third book in the series. This book builds off *The Human Side of Christ* and considers the fact that all people have lost touch with the true human spirit that God gave man when man was created. Man was made in the "image of God." Therefore, imperfections are not a result of being human; rather, humans are not human enough! This book takes the reader on a journey back to our true roots. It provides us a window back in time to view the very first people of God's creation. It also reveals our own souls so we can see the divine creature that lives within each of us.

CPSIA information can be obtained at www.ICGtesting.com
Printed in the USA
BVOW071954281012

304159BV00001B/5/P